Jehovah's Witnesses,

'So-Called'

Jehovah's Witnesses

'SO-CALLED'

Exposing the Errors of the Watch Tower Society

Michael S. Demory

Copyright 2015

ISBN-13: 978-0692336465
ISBN-10: 069233646X

Acknowledgements

A very special note of appreciation is given to those brothers and sisters in Christ who so graciously sacrificed their time and effort to assist me in making sure this book became a reality.

Special thanks to Bryan Hodge, a dear brother in Christ who dedicated many hours proofing this book.

To Jim Mettenbrink, my brother in Christ and faithful gospel preacher who took time out of his busy schedule to help make this book more readable.

To my dear brother Steven Lloyd, whose encouragement and feedback I appreciate beyond words. Having written two books himself, his advice was immeasurable in obtaining the final product.

To my family, who proofed, and edited the book, without your help this book may not have come to fruition.

Thanks to everyone who had a hand in proofing this book, your help has truly been a blessing.

Dedication

To my soul mate
Teresa Demory

My life companion
who captured my heart
the moment I first saw her.
She is my friend, my inspiration,
my fellow-heir of the promise,
who helps keep me grounded in God's way.
She is a wonderful mother who dedicated herself
to homeschooling our children,
and who continues to be a shining example
to them and our grandchildren.
She has been an encouragement to me,
in every aspect of my life.

Table of Contents

"If any man teach otherwise, and consent not to wholesome words, even the words of our Lord Jesus Christ, and to the doctrine which is according to godliness; he is proud, knowing nothing, but doting about questions and strifes of words, whereof cometh envy, strife, railings, evil surmisings, perverse disputings of men of corrupt minds, and destitute of the truth, supposing that gain is godliness."

(1 Timothy 6:3-5)

Preface

The continual reference by the Witnesses that religion and Christendom in general is 'so-called,'[1][2] is the reason why I chose to title this book, "*Jehovah's Witnesses-So-Called.*" The sole purpose for this undertaking is to cause as many as possible to be aware of the inconsistencies and errors set forth by Charles T. Russell - founder of the Watch Tower Bible and Tract Society and International Bible Students; a group that would later be renamed the '*Jehovah's Witnesses*' by Judge Rutherford. There is no denying, that the people identifying themselves as, Jehovah's Witness, are sincere individuals. However sincerity is not enough to save anyone, for the apostle Paul sincerely believed he was performing God's will in persecuting First Century Christians, yet, he discovered he had been sincerely wrong.

The Witnesses are honest people who assume that their way of serving God is the only true way. The Witnesses are correct that denominational Christianity is wrong and that God has chosen only one way of salvation. They accurately understand that the only way of salvation according to God, is for all men and women to live faithfully to the end, and that the multitude of vices accepted by men today are ungodly and no Christian should participate in them. The only reason we are able to

---

[1] J.F. Rutherford, **Reconciliation** (Watch Tower Bible & Tract Society, 1928) pp. 139, 144, 242

[2] J.F. Rutherford, **Government** (Watch Tower Bible & Tract Society, 1928) p. 140

agree with them on these points, is because they have correctly inferred these teachings from God's Word. However, there are a number of issues upon which we cannot agree, because the Witnesses have failed or refused to properly extrapolate God's Word, concerning the doctrines we will set forth herein.

It is out of love for the truth and the souls of all men that this volume is published. The idea behind this study came about when church members began asking how they could answer the Witnesses who knocked their doors. A study of their material ensued to find answers to those questions and it was not long before it was realized how necessary it was to expose the errors that were discovered. My library has volumes of their material which have been acquired over the years, and which helped in a careful study of each of the subjects provided in this volume. I discovered quickly that causal reading of their material was not enough to fully grasp their views, so copious amounts of study were exerted in order to present each lesson without any intended perversion of the beliefs held by the Jehovah's Witnesses. It required months of reading their material then comparing it to the Scriptures, before I was able to begin assembling eight, thirty minute lessons for a weekly television program I produced.

While compiling each lesson, our son-in-law, who was born into a Jehovah's Witness family, began to question his religious beliefs. At my suggestion he compared what the Witnesses teach, with the Scriptures, and began to recognize on his own, numerous inconsistencies. It was not long before he studied himself into obeying the gospel of Christ, thereby putting Him on in baptism (Romans 6:3-6; Galatians 3:27). After the eight television lessons were completed, I was asked if it would be possible to put each lesson in book form. So for this reason it was decided that a transcript of the television lessons would be written so that others could see what is taught by the Witnesses; and hopefully prevent as many as possible from being sucked into the indoctrination of the Watch Tower Society.

Chapter 1

Introduction

"Charge certain men that they teach no other doctrine"
(1 Timothy 1:3)

For decades, men and women have peered from behind curtains to watch couples unloading from vehicles onto their streets, hoping they would not receive a knock on their door. Couples, who represent the sect known as *'The Jehovah's Witnesses.'* Usually in twos, they target street after street, house after house in hopes of converting at least one 'meek' person, [3] due to their obligation to acquire a minimum of ten-hours *'preaching'* per month [see p. 249]. Their dedication is something to be admired, and one that every true follower of Christ should strive to emulate, in taking the unadulterated gospel into a lost and dying world.

Most likely, many reading this book have had the Jehovah's Witnesses knock on their door at one time or another. Most may have ignored them, refusing to answer the door because they were unable to answer their questions, or just didn't want to be bothered by them. Perhaps some have invited them into

---

[3] J.F. Rutherford, **Children** (Watch Tower Bible & Tract Society, 1941) pp. 212, 213

their home because they were either curious about their beliefs, or they were searching for answers.

While they are nice and sincere people, they do not tell the truth about themselves. The only reason for writing this volume, is for the purpose of exposing the errors that the Watch Tower Society teaches and the Jehovah's Witnesses believe. Please keep in mind that exposing the doctrine of the Watch Tower Society does not mean their members are being attacked. Only the beliefs that separate them from God are being exposed for what they truly are - error. Obedience to God should always be the goal of everyone. When He instructs men to do something, they had better do it! Correct (John 14:15; 15:14)? Not only are men commanded by Jesus to believe and teach the same doctrine (John 17:20-21; 1 Corinthians 1:10; et al); Jesus also charges all men to expose anyone that teaches falsely:

> *"And have no fellowship with the unfruitful works of darkness, but rather expose them"* (Ephesians 5:11).

> *"Now I beseech you, brethren, mark them which cause divisions and occasions of stumbling contrary to the doctrine which ye have learned; and avoid them"* (Romans 16:17).

Therefore, in obedience to the Lord Jesus, this volume is set forth for the purpose of exposing the error of the Jehovah's Witnesses. In fact, in their own booklet entitled; *"The Jehovah's Witnesses, Who are They?"* we find this statement:

Introduction

"The Witnesses strongly endorse the course followed by the Bereans when they heard the apostle Paul preach: "They received the word with the greatest eagerness of mind; carefully examining the Scriptures daily as to whether these things were so" (Acts 17:11). **Jehovah's Witnesses believe that all religious teachings should be subjected to this test of agreement with the inspired Scriptures,** *whether the teaching is offered by them or by someone else. They invite you – urge you – to do this."* 4[Emphasis mine]

From their own writings, the Jehovah's Witnesses encourage everyone, to put the doctrine of the Watch Tower Society to the test, which should be the attitude of every religious group that seeks to the truth. Since the goal of this book is to present information about the true teachings of the Jehovah's Witnesses, their materials will be referenced so that their beliefs are not intentionally distorted. The object is to provide information that will help the reader make an informed decision about this group, and their teachings, as well as to what the Bible actually teaches on each subject.

The *'preaching'* 5 performed by the Jehovah's Witnesses is far from the gospel promulgated by the apostles in the first century and faithful Christians since. Theirs is another gospel (Galatians 1:6-9), which is a perverted gospel, that allures the

---

4 Home page of the Watch Tower Website, 2009, and implied in **The Truth that Leads to Eternal Life** (Watch Tower Bible & Tract Society, 1968) p. 13

5 http://en.wikipedia.org/wiki/Jehovah's_Witnesses

materialistic minded. The Jehovah's Witness sect is founded in Calvinism and Premillennialism with a mixture of Buddhism, Hinduism, and Adventism. After parting ways with the Adventists in 1879, the self-proclaimed preacher, Charles Taze Russell, called his new group, *"The International Bible Students."* In the year 1931, the Watch Tower Societies new President, Judge Rutherford, changed their name to *'Jehovah's Witnesses.'* [6]

The majority of their arguments for their beliefs center around the false doctrines of the Roman Catholic Church [7] and Russell's misapplication of Scripture concerning World War I. [8] [9] Like many Protestant Denominations, the Jehovah's Witnesses falsely view the Roman Catholic Church as the 'Mother' church, even though they disagree with many of its doctrines. Russell also believed the *"wars and rumors of wars, nation rising up against nation,"* that Jesus warned of in Matthew chapter Twenty-Four referred to World War I.

Their reasoning against the doctrines of the Trinity, the immoral soul and Hell, is because the Catholic Church teaches it, which is absolutely irrational on its face. All religious doctrine must be compared to the Word of God, not what other men believe or think.

Russell believed and taught that the *'Witnesses'* had existed

---

[6] **Jehovah's Witnesses Proclaimers of God's Kingdom** (Watch Tower Bible & Tract Society, 1993) pp. 155, 156

[7] J.F. Rutherford, **Riches** (Watch Tower Bible & Tract Society, 1936) pp. 206, 208

[8] J.F. Rutherford, **Government** (Watch Tower Bible & Tract Society, 1928) pp. 170, 173

[9] J.F. Rutherford, **Prophecy** (Watch Tower Bible & Tract Society, 1929), p. 76

since the days of Abel, as he argued that the Scriptures say;

> *"By faith Abel offered unto God a more excellent sacrifice than Cain, by which he obtained* **witness** *that he was righteous, God testifying of his gifts: and by it being dead yet speaketh."* (Hebrews 11:4) [Emphasis mine].

In short, the Watch Tower Society teaches it was God's original intent that Adam and Eve be fruitful and multiply, so that all humanity would live on paradise earth (Eden), and proclaim the name of Jehovah for all eternity. They claim, however, that because the devil did not want Jehovah's name proclaimed, he deceived Eve, causing Adam to sin so that both would be banished from the Garden. Because the pair chose to forfeit their '*Perfect Human Life*' [see p. 248] in paradise, Jehovah punished them with annihilation upon their physical death, with no future hope of a cloned resurrection.

According to the Witnesses, the '*seed*' referred to in the prophecy of Genesis 3:15, denotes the Devil's organization (Civil Government and Religion) vs. God's Government (The Watch Tower Bible and Tract Society and the Christ) [see 'The Seed,' and 'The Christ,' pp. 254, 258]. They contend that God created the Logos (Jesus) in the beginning to become the savior of His Predestined organization (Ephesians 1:5); an organization that would save the world. The Watch Tower Society contends that Jehovah's Witnesses have existed since Abel, but died out after the apostles were killed. They maintain that in 1880 God raised up Charles T. Russell (a type of

Daniel), to rekindle God's organization (the Watch Tower Society), thereby fulfilling prophecy and preparing the world for the Battle of Armageddon [see p. 227].

It is believed the Witnesses, that God pre-chose in eternity an elect group (144,000), who, along with Jesus, would comprise '*the Christ*' (the Church of Christ) in heaven. This special group composes the governing board of the Watch Tower Bible and Tract Society (God's organization/government). They believe this organization was established by Jehovah to properly interpret the Scriptures, and to reveal '*new light*' [see p. 245] to its members. The Witnesses firmly believe that the end of the world was supposed to come in the year 1914, when the Battle of Armageddon was supposed to destroy Satan's organization (Denominations, the nations, and world rulers), thereby ushering in the Millennial reign of '*the Christ*' (144,000 + Jesus); and thereby giving all but Adam & Eve a second chance to become God's chosen (a Jehovah's Witness).

Regrettably, they still await the fulfillment of that prophecy, having changed the year for Armageddon a dozen or more times. They teach that everyone resurrected after Armageddon will be clones of their former selves. Should anyone fail the millennial test period within the first one hundred years, they will suffer the '*second death*' [see p. 257] and his clone will be erased from God's memory banks forever. Those who pass the millennial testing will be granted eternal life on earth with those Jehovah's Witnesses who escaped Armageddon (their idea of salvation).

The reason why Jehovah's Witnesses knock doors, is in keeping with their idea of *'preaching.'* Their goal is to save *'persons of good will'* (those gullible enough to accept their doctrine) [see p. 257 – The Meek] from the Battle of Armageddon. They contend that the gospel will not be preached for the saving of the individual until the Millennial reign. This was certainly shock the apostle Paul who said over and over again that he preached the gospel, because it was God's power to save (1 Corinthians 1:17; Galatians 1:11; Romans 1:16). Any honest Bible Student understands that God's Word is without contradiction (1 Corinthians 14:33).

Only through twisting the Scriptures (2 Peter 3:16) was Charles Russell able to invent a religion that is not a thirty-second cousin to the Christianity God intended (Ephesians 1:4-10). Just because Jesus told His disciples they would be His *"Witnesses,"* does not mean that they would be of the *'Jehovah's Witness'* sect, as the Watch Tower Society claims is the case (Hebrews 11:4 – 12:1). Their misunderstanding of the kingdom of God teaches that the kingdom is not the church, because according to them, the church is nothing more than Catholicism gone to seed. According to the Witnesses, the church does not reside on earth, but is composed of Jesus and the 144,000 in heaven, which they refer to as 'The Christ,' the only ones who are truly born again.

Because the teachings of the Witnesses are in constant flux, it is sometimes difficult to pin them down as to what they really believe – which is true of all groups that believe they receive new revelation from God. When studying with the Witnesses, one might point out a certain contradiction in one of their doctrines, to which they will answer that '*new light*' has caused them to modify their belief in that particular doctrine. When this book goes to print, more '*new light*' will no doubt have been received that will make it appear that what has been revealed in this book is false. The only way to counter their answers of receiving '*new light*,' is to know what they teach by accumulating their materials. Then, when a supposed contradiction appears, their own recent writings can be used against them.

The Witnesses are shrewd in the way they use the phrase, '*new light*,' because the reality is, they still believe whatever doctrine is in question, while pretending not to. In many ways, '*new light*' has just become their way of shutting down a conversation that reveals their false doctrine and prophecies. One such change will be discussed in the appendix under the heading '*God's Organization*' [see pp. 175 & 237]. It is my hope that this volume will enlighten everyone concerning the teachings of the Witnesses, as well as prevent future converts to a religion that is unable to save one soul.

Summary

The purpose of this book is to expose the errors taught by the Watch Tower Society, and believed by its members, the Jehovah's Witnesses. The Watch Tower Society contends that God created the Logos (Jesus), to become the savior of God's predestined organization – The Watch Tower Society. At one time, only the select group of 144,000 Witnesses are allowed to govern the board of the Society and to properly interpret the Scriptures, but *new light* now allows the average Witness to serve on the board.

Chapter 2

The Origins of the
Jehovah's Witnesses

*"I marvel that you are so soon removed from Him that called
into the grace of Christ unto another gospel: which is not
another gospel; but there are some that trouble you, and
would pervert the gospel of Christ."*
(Galatians 1:6-7)

Who are the Jehovah's Witnesses? Where did they come from? Are they the true church Jesus said He would build? Scripture points out that Jesus clearly stated He would build HIS church [singular] (Matthew 16:18), thereby being the one and only founder (1 Corinthians 3:11). Most agree that the church began in Jerusalem on Pentecost 30AD (Acts 2), yet we find a difference between the church Jesus said He would build and the one the Witnesses and all other denominations claim.

The Watch Tower Bible and Tract Society was first founded by William Conley in 1881 with Charles Russell as secretary-treasurer. It was incorporated on December 15, 1884 as *"Zion's Watch Tower Tract Society"* with Russell named as President. In 1896 the Society was renamed, *"Watch Tower Bible and Tract Society,"* with the final change in 1955 to *"Watch Tower Bible and Tract Society of Pennsylvania."* All this was executed so that the Witnesses were not relying upon commercial printers to print their material. The Watch Tower Society determines everything the Jehovah's Witnesses are required to believe and teach.

Their argument for this arrangement is like that of the Roman Catholic Church – their members are not smart enough to understand the Bible, so they must study only that which their headquarters deems to be doctrinal material. The Watch Tower Society writes all the study material and sends it to each congregation to be studied. On any given Sunday, Jehovah's Witnesses around the world will open the same study material and study the same lesson. They argue that it is for the purpose of agreeing together on doctrine, yet despite their reasoning, the truth is, that Witnesses from different Kingdom Halls do not always agree.

Please take note that there is nothing at all inappropriate with seeking to be united in doctrine, for Jesus commanded **all** His followers to believe and teach the same thing (doctrine).

*"Now I beseech you, brethren, by the name of the Lord Jesus Christ, that you all speak the same thing, and that there be **no divisions** among you; but that you be perfectly joined together in the same mind and in the same judgment"* (1 Corinthians 1:10) [Emphasis mine]

*"There should be **no schism** (division) in the body;.."* (1 Corinthians 12:25) [Emphasis mine]

*"Nevertheless, whereto we have already attained, let us **walk by the same rule**, let us mind the same thing"* (Philippians 3:16) [Emphasis mine]

However, it is apparent that the motivation for the Watch Tower Society, or anyone else establishing such a rule, is so that the doctrines of men take precedence over God's doctrine. This must be true, because Witnesses – like Catholics are not allowed to read the material of others. They are not allowed to think for themselves. They like Catholics must accept without question every doctrine taught by headquarters. While they claim to be people of the Bible, in reality they are people of the Watch Tower Society, like Catholics are people of the Vatican, and Mormons are people of Salt Lake City. Listen to the words of the Watch Tower.

"...people cannot see the Divine plan in studying the Bible by itself...if he then lays them [Scripture Studies] aside and ignores them and goes to the Bible alone, though he has understood his Bible for ten years, our experience shows that within two years he goes into darkness. On the other hand, if he had merely read the Scriptures Studies with their references, and had not read a page of the Bible, as such, he would be in the light at the end of the two years, because he would have the light of the Scriptures." [10]

"We all need help to understand the Bible, and we

---

[10] **Watch Tower Magazine**, (Watch Tower Bible & Tract Society, September 15, 1910) p. 298

cannot find the Scriptural guidance we need outside the 'faithful and discreet slave' organization." [11]

"The world is full of Bibles, which Book contains the commandments of God. Why, then, do the people not know which way to go? Because they do not also have the teaching or law of the mother, which is light. Jehovah God has provided his holy written Word for all mankind and it contains all the information that is needed for men in taking a course leading to life. But God has not arranged for that Word to speak independently or to shine forth life-giving truths by itself. His Word says: "Light is sown for the righteous." (Ps. 97:11). It is through his organization that God provides this light that the proverb says is the teaching or law of the mother. If we are to walk in the light of truth we must recognize not only Jehovah God as our Father but his organization as our mother." [12]

Notice if you will that the Witnesses believe the Watch Tower Bible and Tract Society is the *'mother'* from whom all understanding of God's Word must come. Without it, men will not obtain life-giving light. Isn't that what the Roman Catholic Church tells its members? Was not also the same true of Jim Jones & David Koresh? Nowhere in God's Word, do we find an example of Christians being instructed to follow the dictates of some organization or individual. Everyone is commanded to

---

[11] **Watch Tower Magazine**, (Watch Tower Bible & Tract Society, February 15, 1981)

[12] **Watch Tower Magazine**, (Watch Tower Bible & Tract Society, May 1, 1957) p 274

follow Jesus and His word alone (John 14:15; 15:14; 1 John 5:3; Hebrews 5:9; Galatians 1:6-9).

Before the year 1931 the name '*Jehovah's Witness*' [see p. 242], was unknown. From their inception until 1931 they were simply known as '*International Bible Students.*' The Witnesses assert they have been around since the days of Abel, but they must twist the Scriptures to make their point. Their favorite text used to show the unsuspecting they are God's true people, is the book of Hebrews chapter eleven. *"By faith Abel offered unto God a more excellent sacrifice than Cain, by which he obtained <u>witness</u> that he was righteous..."* (Hebrews 11:4). It is a perversion of Scripture to pull out a word and define it in a way not intended by the author. This verse and others like it, are not teaching men were '*Jehovah's Witnesses.*' They are simply pointing out the fact that their '*faith*' became a '*witness*' or '*testimony*' to their righteousness. If it is true that Jehovah's Witnesses have always been part of God's eternal plan, and that Abel was the first to be considered a '*Jehovah's Witness*' then why did Russell not name them so from the very beginning? After all, Charles Taze Russell is the proclaimed founder of the Jehovah's Witnesses, is he not?

The problem with false doctrine is that the men that invent them must always find passages of Scripture that appear to back them up. This method of interpretation is referred to as '*eisegesis,*' – reading into a verse what you want it to say, rather than the proper way of interpretation, which is '*exegesis,*' gleaning out of the passage what the author meant to say. The word '*witness*' in Hebrews 11:4 does not refer to a religious sect, but to the actions of Abel and others that proved their faith was genuine.

Russell was raised a Presbyterian, but joined the Congregational Church at the age of thirteen. At the age of sixteen he began to question his beliefs and dabbled in Islam, Buddhism, Hinduism and other religious philosophies. By the age of eighteen, Russell met an Adventist preacher, and became interested in his prophesies concerning the second coming (advent) of Christ. Over the next nine years Russell immersed himself in Adventist doctrine, as well as continuing his studies on Pyramidology.

According to Russell, the Great Pyramid of Giza [13] held many Bible truths that would help men understand God's timeline of the kingdom. His beliefs about the Great Pyramid, plus his false interpretations from the book of Daniel is where he obtained his ideas about the years 1874, 1878, 1881, 1910 and 1914. Regrettably, due to their poor hermeneutical methods, most all denominations teach falsely regarding the book of Daniel. In 1879 Russell parted ways with the Adventists because he disagreed with their prophetic assumptions – and rightly so! In reality the Jehovah's Witnesses are nothing more than a splinter group of the Adventists [14] of which there are several, each having split over differing dates concerning the return (advent) of Christ.

Russell believed and taught that Christ began His '*invisible*

[13] Charles T. Russell, **The Divine Plan of the Ages**, (The Dawn Bible Students Association, 1916) pp. 82, 83

[14] **Jehovah's Witnesses-Proclaimers of God's Kingdom**, (Watch Tower Bible & Tract Society, 1993) pp. 46, 47

presence' in 1874. [15] Please keep in mind that in order for anyone to become a *'Bible Student,'* they were required to believe in, and confess agreement with the 1874 date. In other words, a person must believe that Christ <u>began</u> His invisible presence in 1874, (a date that was later changed to 1914) as well as believe and confess that as a 'Bible Student' he would inherit the earth which is the only true kingdom of God. Mr. Russell also taught that in 1878 [16] Christ <u>began</u> to reign over His kingdom, and that the year 1881 [17] marked the last opportunity for the Bible Students to become part of the 'elect class' or the 144,000 [see p. 260].

In the beginning this was not a problem, since there were less than 144,000 *'Bible Students'* world-wide. However, *'new light'* caused Judge Rutherford to teach that 1935 [see p. 232], would be the final date for acceptance into the elect class. When their numbers grew beyond 144,000, Rutherford obtained *'new light'* again, that revealed every baptized Jehovah's Witness after 1935 could only become a part of a new class - the *'Great Crowd'* class.

Judge Rutherford stated in his book entitled *"Children,"* on page 185: *"Aside from those who compose the "Little Flock" there are human creatures that get life everlasting and must*

---

[15] Charles T. Russell, 1916, **Studies in the Scriptures** Vol. 2, Study VI, Great Jubilee Began (Watch Tower Bible & Tract Society, 1874) pp. B193-200

[16] Charles T. Russell, **Studies in the Scriptures** 1916, Vol. 3, Study VI, The Testing and Sifting of the Sanctuary Class, p. C189

[17] Charles T. Russell, **Studies in the Scriptures** Vol. 3, Study VI, The End of the High Calling, (Watch Tower Bible & Tract Society, 1916) pp. C213, 214 – and **Millennial Dawn:** The Time is At Hand, (Watch Tower Bible & Tract Society, 1889) p. 235

live on the earth. Such human creatures, pictured by this "Other Sheep" cannot go to heaven, and therefore must find life on earth." He said that those inheriting the earth will be of the *'great crowd'* class, but those who inherit heaven will be made up of the 144,000 only – the *'Little Flock'* class, who are also called the *'elect'* or *'Kingdom Class.'* [18] This however was not so according to Russell, the founder of the Watch Tower sect. Russell saw <u>all</u> Witnesses as the *'little flock'* [see p. 243], who would inherit heaven. It was Rutherford who modified their doctrine when the number of Witnesses grew past 144,000. It is interesting that in recent years the Watch Tower Society has reverted to the original teaching of their founder. (see new light, p. 245 & 185)

Russell taught that in 1910 [19] the tribulation would begin with the Battle of Armageddon, which Battle would occur in the year 1914, with the complete establishment of the kingdom of God on earth. When Charles Russell died in October of 1916, the Watch Tower leadership were unsure who should lead them. In January of 1917, they elected J.F. (Self-proclaimed Judge) Rutherford as their new President. [20] Rutherford had joined the Bible Students in 1906 and was appointed their legal counsel in 1907. Upon becoming President he began making sweeping changes to their organization and teachings; which caused extensive division among the ranks and eventually the loss of thousands of Bible Students.

---

[18] **The Truth that Leads to Eternal Life**, (Watch Tower Bible & Tract Society, 1968) pp. 76, 77

[19] Charles T. Russell, **Millennial Dawn**: Vol. 3, Thy Kingdom Come, (Watch Tower Bible & Tract Society, 1891) p. 664

[20] Ibid, p. 68

Several different groups broke away from the Russellites to form their own groups, in order to maintain the teachings of Charles Russell. Groups as, The Dawn Bible Students Association; Laymen's Home Missionary Movement; Pastoral Bible Institute; and the Standfast Movement - these last two groups having ceased to exist. Judge Rutherford claimed the Watch Tower Society as his, and in 1931 [see p. 232], renamed the group once known as the Bible Students, to the Jehovah's Witnesses. So it was Judge Rutherford, not Charles Russell or even Jehovah God who is responsible for the Jehovah's Witness name.

Under Rutherford, several changes were made, and like the Catholic Church, they claim their changes came from God through new revelations (*new light*). [21] Rutherford stopped all references to the great pyramid, and denounced it as the teachings of Satan. One must question how this could be possible, if it is true that the Watch Tower Society is really God's organization? Since we are told that God does not lie, nor is He the author of confusion (Titus 1:2; 1 Corinthians 14:33); then the doctrines Rutherford changed should have stood.

Next, Rutherford changed the dates established by Russell. He moved the invisible presence of Christ from 1874 to 1914, [22] which then required the final year of the Jehovah's Witnesses being able to become part of the elect class/144,000 from 1881

---

[21] **Watch Tower Magazine**, (Watch Tower Bible & Tract Society, April 1, 1972) pp. 197, 198, 199

[22] J.F. Rutherford, **Golden Age Magazine** (Watch Tower Bible & Tract Society, 1930) p. 503

to 1935. [23] Again, how is this possible if God is really the source of their '*light?*' After 1935, the gates of heaven were closed and all future Jehovah's Witnesses could only hope to be preserved from the Battle of Armageddon (their plan of salvation), and to live eternally upon the earth.

According to the Watch Tower Society, which is supposed to receive its orders directly from God, the governing body of the Society must be composed entirely of the '*Elect Class*' alone. Only those who were living in 1914 are allowed to govern the Watch Tower Society and establish doctrine, because they alone are approved of God as the elect. Consider, if you will, the ramifications of this requirement. What happens, when all those of the '*Elect Class*' are dead, when there is no one left alive who lived in 1914, and the prophecies have not yet come to pass? Do the Jehovah's Witnesses just close their doors since no doctrine will be forthcoming? Or will they receive '*new light*' which will change that requirement?

Like all date setters, they must either change their dates, or admit they are false prophets. However, knowing they will never admit they are false prophets, suggests they will require a change in their dates, and board requirements. As the Jehovah's Witnesses have done so many times before concerning their date for the end of the world, when the end did not arrive in 1914, [24] like Russell predicted – they changed

---

[23] J.F. Rutherford, **Let God be True**, (Watch Tower Bible & Tract Society,1946) p. 298; and **Jehovah's Witnesses in the Divine Purpose**, (Watch Tower Bible & Tract Society, 1959) p. 139; and, **Revelation, its Grand Climax Now at Hand**, (Watch Tower Bible & Tract Society, 1988) p. 125

[24] **Watch Tower Magazine**, (Watch Tower Bible & Tract Society, June 15, 1911) p. 190

the date. Or when it didn't come in 1918 as Rutherford said it would - and again in 1925, [25] in 1975, [26] and in 1995. [27] Based upon their track record, why should anyone trust anything they say? If God is truly behind them then He would surely give them the correct date (Deuteronomy 13:1-5; 18:15-22).

The Watch Tower Society of Jehovah's Witnesses are comprised of several levels within their organization. There is the *'Elect Class'* which is referred to as the 144,000 who Jehovah has already chosen. This group of Jehovah's Witnesses alone is born again, having received the benefits of Jesus' death upon the cross, thereby being promised a heavenly home. It is from this elect class that the Watch Tower Society and its Governing Board consist and which provides *'spiritual food'* (doctrine & teaching) to all their congregations world-wide.

Under the oversight of the Governing Body originate the Branch offices, referred to as *'Bethels,'* of which there are 91 worldwide. Each *'Bethel'* is overseen by a committee of 3 or more elders who have been appointed by the Governing Body. Congregations of Jehovah's Witnesses are composed of 10-200 members who meet in *'Kingdom Halls'* and reside in their congregational territory. Kingdom Halls are often shared by 2 or more congregations, with each congregation being overseen by their own elders and meeting at different times.

---

[25] **Watch Tower Magazine**, (Watch Tower Bible & Tract Society, May 15, 1922) p. 147

[26] **Watch Tower Magazine**, (Watch Tower Bible & Tract Society, July 1, 1979) p. 29

[27] **Watch Tower Magazine**, (Watch Tower Bible & Tract Society, December 15, 2003) p. 15

Next we find the *'Great Crowd/Multitude Class'* [28] or *'Other Sheep Class'* [see p. 247], which comprises the reminder of the Jehovah's Witnesses. As a member of the *'Other Sheep'* a person will start out as an 'Associate' who is also referred to as a *'Bible Student.'* A Bible Student (Watch Tower Student) is a person or family who is involved in weekly studies (Watch Tower doctrine) with the Jehovah's Witnesses in their home. Before anyone is allowed to *'join'* the Jehovah's Witnesses, they must have gone through the Witnesses complete study course AND be an active *'associate'* (Bible Student) who regularly attends their meetings and demonstrates interest in learning more (being indoctrinated in Watch Tower doctrine) as well as being involved in their activities. [29]

Should anyone decide they want to become an active Jehovah's Witness, he must meet with the elders. They will make sure the new prospect truly believes their doctrines, as he will be required to confess his belief in the invisible kingdom, and that it came about in the year 1914. He will be required to commit himself to active door knocking, and weekly Bible study (Watch Tower study). When the elders are convinced of his beliefs and commitment, he will be allowed to be baptized [see p. 228], into the Jehovah's Witnesses.

Now he is considered a *'Baptized Publisher'* or *'Ordained Minister'* meaning he must knock doors. This door knocking to spread their propaganda is called 'Preaching.' He will be required to dedicate no less than ten hours per month, to be

---

[28] J.F. Rutherford, **Riches** (Watch Tower Bible & Tract Society, 1936) p. 294
[29] http://en.wikipedia.org/wiki/Organizational_structure_of_Jehovah's_Witnesses

considered a regular publisher, or fifty hours per month of *'preaching,'* if you want to be a *'publisher'* in good standing among the Jehovah's Witnesses. From what I have researched, it is my understanding that this varies from congregation to congregation and how demanding the elders are. Their *'ordained minister's'* are divided into categories such as, Auxiliary Pioneers, Regular Pioneers, Special Pioneers and Missionaries, depending upon the number of hours one is willing to dedicate to *'preaching.'* Special Pioneers and Missionaries must dedicate 140 hours per month to preaching, while Regular Pioneers must spent 70 hours or more. [30]

Every Witness is required to keep track of every door they knock and the hours spent *'preaching,'* which is then handed over to their elders. The rules for counting hours preached are diverse, depending upon whether it is *'informal witnessing,'* *'field service,'* or *'Bible Study.'* Concerning *'field service,'* Witnesses are not allowed to count their time until they have actually knocked a door. Their time stops when they leave a door to walk to the next door or when taking a break. However, they can make up their time through *'informal witnessing,'* which takes place with anyone who comes across their path (co-workers, shopping, etc.).

Should the elders find that you are not meeting your quota, you may be marked irregular and face additional indoctrination. Within each congregation are 'overseers' who are appointed to ensure proper care of the congregation. These men serve as *'presiding overseer, secretary, service overseer,*

---

[30] **Jehovah's Witnesses Branch Organization Manual**, 2003 Edition, p. 117

Watch Tower Study conductor, Congregation Book Study overseer, and Theocratic Ministry School overseer.' The elders are responsible for public talks, teaching the congregation and leading field ministry. [31]

Jehovah's Witnesses meet no less than five times a week for Bible study (Watch Tower indoctrination). Everything you study is preplanned by the Watch Tower Society. They contend that its purpose is when you are traveling you can know you will study the same lesson on the road that you would at home. That certainly sounds innocent enough, but in reality it is nothing more than forced feeding of Jehovah's Witness doctrine. Remember, we said the Jehovah's Witnesses are not allowed to read any religious material that doesn't come from the Watch Tower Society Headquarters. Anyone caught doing so, will face possible disfellowship. [32]

When studying with Jehovah's Witnesses you must be aware that they have a different definition of words than most Christians do. They will talk to you about Jesus, about His death upon the cross, about His atonement [see p. 228], and about the gospel [see p. 256], however, they do not mean it in the same way you understand it to imply. This is also true of Mormons. To the Jehovah's Witnesses, the gospel does not apply to all people. When they speak of the gospel, they are referring to the kingdom message that will be preached after the millennial kingdom is established following the Battle of

---

[31] **Organized to do Jehovah's Will** (Watch Tower Bible and Tract Society, 2005) pp. 29, 40, 41, 42

[32] **Organized to do Jehovah's Will**, (Watch Tower Bible & Tract Society, 2005) pp. 28, 44, 81, 87-91, 112-113, 180-218

Armageddon, not according to what the Bible actually teaches about the gospel. Their gospel teaches that Jesus was enthroned invisibly in 1914, which is quite a different message than what Paul preached.

> *"But we preached Christ crucified, unto the Jews a stumbling block, and unto the Greeks foolishness; but unto them which are called, both Jews and Greeks, Christ the power of God, and the wisdom of God"* (1 Corinthians 1:23-24).

> *"Now I make known unto you brethren, the gospel which I preached unto you, which also ye received, wherein also ye stand, by which also ye are saved, if ye hold fast the word which I preached unto you, except ye believed in vain. For I delivered unto you first of all that which also I received: that Christ died for our sins according to the scriptures; and that he was buried; and that he hath been raised on the third day according to the scriptures;"* (1 Cor 15:1-4ASV)

Like Calvinists who believe in limited atonement, Jehovah's Witnesses believe Christ's atonement is limited to the 'Elect Class' – the 144,000. [33] Based upon their false view of the gospel, that it refers to the invisible kingdom of Christ in 1914, what historical or Scriptural proof do they provide? None! If it is the case that Jesus <u>began</u> an invisible presence in the year 1914, then why did John say that when Jesus returned "*<u>EVERY</u>*

---

[33] Charles T. Russell, **The Divine Plan of the Ages**, (The Dawn Bible Students Association,1916) pp. 152, 153

eye would see Him" (Revelation 1:7)? If God doesn't mean what He says in His inspired Word, then we should just throw the Bible out and believe whatever we want to believe; which is apparently what the Jehovah's Witnesses have done when it comes to Christ's return.

Then we are told by the Witnesses that Jesus didn't reign until 1914, yet the apostles understood that Jesus began His reign in 30AD when He ascended into heaven:

> *"Men and brethren, let me freely speak unto you of the patriarch David, that he is both dead and buried, and his sepulcher is with us unto this day. Therefore being a prophet, and knowing that God had sworn with an oath to him, that of the fruit of his loins, according to the flesh, he would raise up Christ to sit on his throne; he seeing this before spake of the resurrection of Christ, that his soul was not left in Hades, neither his flesh did see corruption. This Jesus hath God raised up, whereof we all are witnesses. Therefore being by the right hand of God exalted, and having received of the Father the promise of the Holy Spirit, he hath shed forth this which you now see and hear. For David is not ascended into the heavens: but he saith himself, the Lord said unto my Lord, Sit thou on my right hand."* (Acts 2:29-34)

The apostle Paul in making his argument for the death and resurrection of Jesus Christ said that Jesus would reign UNTIL His second coming.

*"But now is Christ risen from the dead, and become the firstfruits of them that slept. For since by man came death, by man came also the resurrection of the dead. For as in Adam all die, even so in Christ shall all be made alive. But every man in his own order: Christ the firstfruits; afterward they that are Christ's at His coming, then cometh the end, when He shall have delivered up the kingdom to God, even the Father; when He shall have put down all rule and all authority and power. For **He MUST REIGN, <u>TILL</u>** He hath put all enemies under His feet. The last enemy that shall be destroyed is death."* (1 Corinthians 15:20-26) [Emphasis mine]

Who are we to believe, the Watch Tower Society or God? Christ's kingdom exists now, over which Jesus now reigns as king, and has been reigning since His ascension into heaven in the First Century AD. When He returns, Jesus will judge everyone and divide the sheep from the goats (Matthew 25:31-46); at which point He will return the kingdom to its rightful owner – God the Father (1 Corinthians 15:24). There should be no misunderstanding, because the Bible is very clear in its teaching – there was no invisible return of Christ, nor will there be. Therefore, this particular doctrine of the Jehovah's Witnesses fails, and if one fails, then their entire house of cards fails.

It is very likely that everyone has heard many churches make the claim that they are the one and only true church; which is something the Witnesses sincerely believe about themselves, as do the Mormons, Catholics, Baptists, et al. Scripture informs us that God established only one approved religious group in the world, but it is not the Jehovah's Witnesses any more than it is the Mormons or the Roman Catholic Church. God did the same thing in the Old Testament; by choosing out of all the nations in the world only '*one*' (the Israelites). The same continues to be true today. There is only one religious group authorized by God to exist. After Jesus established His one and only church in 30AD which was commanded to spread the truth (Matthew 16:18; Acts 2:47; Mark 16:-15-16), men began to teach their own brand of religion – fulfilling the prophecy of apostasy.

> *"Now the Spirit speaketh expressly, that in the latter times some shall depart from the faith, giving heed to seducing spirits, and doctrines of devils; speaking lies in hypocrisy; having their conscience seared with a hot iron; forbidding to marry, to abstain from meats, which God hath created to be received with thanksgiving of them that believe and know the truth. Every creature of God is good, and nothing to be refused, if it be received with thanksgiving;"* (1 Timothy 4:1-4).

> *"But there were false prophets also among the people, even as there shall be false teachers among you, who privily shall bring in destructive heresies, even denying the Lord that bought them, and bring upon themselves swift destruction"* (2 Peter 2:1)

"Let no man deceive you by any means: for that day shall not come, except there come a falling away first, and that man of sin be revealed, the son of perdition;" (2 Thessalonians 2:3)

From the beginning, the world has been drinking up the devil's Kool-Aid (Revelation 12:15-16), and the Jehovah's Witnesses are definitely among the multitude of gullible drinkers. God has always had a pattern, a blueprint for men to follow. He gave Noah a blueprint concerning the construction of the Ark, and Noah followed it precisely (Genesis 6:22). Noah had no authority from God to choose any other wood than gopher wood. Had he chosen to change God's blueprint, Noah and his family would have drown, like everyone else. Moses was given a blueprint for the building of the Tabernacle (Hebrews 8:5). Moses followed that pattern precisely and was pleasing to God. The same is true for Christ's church today. There is a pattern, a blueprint. It is the New Testament. If we follow exactly what the first century Christians did, we will have the same church as they had – the church of Christ – NOT the Kingdom Hall or the Jehovah's Witnesses or any other denominational group.

God's law of sowing and reaping is just as viable in nature as it is in the spiritual world (Genesis 1:11-12). According to the parable of the sower, the '*seed*' is the Word of God (Luke 8:11-15). When sown in the hearts of open and honest individuals, it will produce a Christian, and only a Christian. We find no such animal as a hyphenated Christian in the Bible, yet today men have accepted such as God approved. Luke said they were first called *"Christians"* at Antioch (Acts 26), not Jehovah's

Witnesses, or any other man invented name. Those Christians of the First Century were added to Christ's one and only church by God, when they obeyed God's prerequisites to salvation (Acts 2:38-47).

The Jehovah's Witnesses have not followed the New Testament pattern. They have followed the pattern of Charles Taze Russell and Judge Rutherford. The church Jesus built was founded by Jesus Christ.

> *"And Simon Peter answered and said, Thou art the Christ, the Son of the living God. And Jesus answered and said unto him, Blessed art thou, Simon Bar-jona: for flesh and blood hath not revealed it unto thee, but My Father which is in heaven. And I say also unto thee, that thou are Peter, and upon this rock I will build My church; and the gates of Hades shall not prevail against it"* (Matthew 16:16-18)

> *"For other foundation can no man lay than that is laid, which is Jesus Christ"* (1 Corinthians 3:11).

The church Jesus built was founded in Jerusalem in 30AD as foretold in prophecy (Isaiah 2:1-2; Luke 24:46-49). The Jehovah's Witnesses do not meet the pattern/blueprint, and the same is true of every denomination. The Jehovah's Witnesses began in 1931 in Pittsburgh, Pennsylvania after Judge Rutherford changed their name from 'The Bible Students.' Therefore, the Jehovah's Witnesses have the wrong founder, the wrong founding date and wrong founding place.

They have no authority from God to exist, and therefore are another device of the devil to capture the souls of men. The Jehovah's Witnesses are also not from God because they teach a multitude of falsehoods.

They do not believe in the atoning power of Christ's blood to remit sin. Consider what they say about Jesus' sacrifice in their book entitled "*Salvation*" on page 173:

> "*When Jesus Christ was exalted to heaven he presented to God in heaven <u>the value of his human life;</u> and that asset, which was exactly equal to what Adam had forfeited, was received by Jehovah God as the offering of Jesus for sin, that is to say as the purchase price offered and presented by Jesus in behalf of sinful men*" [Emphasis mine]

They do not believe we have an eternal soul, nor do they believe in the existence of an eternal hell. In 1946 the Watchtower Society wrote the following:

> "*The devil is the one that originated the doctrine of the inherent immortality of the soul.*" [34]

According to Judge Rutherford:

> "*Hell is not a place, it is a condition of death. That is to say, in the condition of death or out of existence*" [35]

---

[34] **Let God be True**, (Watch Tower Bible & Tract Society, 1946) p. 66, 67
[35] [35] J.F. Rutherford, **Reconciliation** (Watch Tower Bible & Tract Society, 1928) p. 296

They do not believe that Jesus is God, and they believe that the Holy Spirit is nothing more than electricity. Rutherford also says:

> *"As for the Holy Spirit, the so-called third person of the trinity, we have already seen that IT is not a person, but God's active force."* [36]

The Watch Tower Society is composed of false prophets whose prophecies have not come to pass. They have a system of works salvation akin to the Roman Catholic Church. Remember, the Jehovah's Witnesses are required to knock doors (preach) a minimum of ten hours per month, to be considered in good standing. The elders keep track of their works, and if they are not doing as the elders think they should, the Witness may be disciplined. Jehovah's Witnesses are not allowed to salute the flag, pledge alliance to the flag, vote or hold public office. [37] Jehovah's Witnesses and their family members are not allowed to give blood, or to have blood transfusions of any type, which includes platelets. [38]

That's right, if a Witness or any member of their family requires blood in surgery or for any other reason, they can't have it! If they do, they will be kicked out of the Jehovah's Witnesses. They can't even store their own blood for future use, or donate blood to someone in need, including family members. That is not allowed in the Jehovah's Witnesses.

---

[36] Ibid, p. 296

[37] Jehovah's Witness Website, JW.org/ FAQ

[38] **What Does the Bible Really Teach**, (Watch Tower Bible & Tract Society, 2005) pp. 128-131

Jehovah's Witnesses are materialists, who believe the earth will last forever, and that it will belong to them alone. All of the information that has been provided about the Jehovah's Witnesses has come from their own material. The purpose of this book is not to demean the men and women who consider themselves Jehovah's Witnesses; it is to expose their false doctrines, doctrines that they will not tell a prospect about when they knock on their door. They will use words and phrases that most are familiar with, but words and phrases that will have a totally different meaning to them. Beware of this group and their teachings.

Summary

Charles Taze Russell founded the religious group known as the *'International Bible Students.'* They were not known as *'Jehovah's Witnesses'* until 1931 when J.F. Rutherford, President of the Watch Tower Bible and Tract Society received *'new light'* concerning their name. On December 15, 1884, The Watch Tower Bible & Tract Society was incorporated, with Charles Russell as its President.

Witnesses believe the WTBTS is the *'mother'* from whom all understanding of God's Word must flow. Russell taught that in 1878 Christ began to reign over His kingdom invisibly, and that the year 1881 marked the last opportunity for the Bible Students to be added to the 144,000. However, Rutherford received *'new light'* and changed the date to 1935. Since 1935, only members of the Elect Class (144,000) have been allowed to govern the Watch Tower Society and determine doctrine and teachings; but that requirement changed in 2012 when they received 'new light.'

The Witnesses do not believe in the atoning power of Christ's blood to remit the sins of the world; they do not believe Jesus or the Holy Spirit are God; or that each of us possesses an immortal soul. The average Witness is considered an ordained minister who is required to preach (knock doors) a minimum of ten (10) hours per month.

Questions to Consider

1. Who is the founder of the church, Jesus said He would build?

2. Where and when was Christ's church founded?

3. List the who, where, and when for the Jehovah's Witnesses and compare the list to the Bible.

4. Does God authorize divisions in the church? If not, does the Bible provide answers on how to prevent division? List some passages for your answers.

5. Does any earthly organization have the authority to dictate doctrine? If not, list passages that prove they do not.

6. Are Christians commanded to preach the gospel? If so, list passages for your answers.

7. Are Christians required by God to commit a minimum of 10 hours a month for evangelism? If not, how must time should they dedicate?

Chapter 3

The Trinity

"For there are three that bear record in heaven, the Father,
the Word, and the Holy Spirit: and these three are one."
(1 John 5:7)

Very little of what the Jehovah's Witnesses believe is taught in the Bible (KJV, et al). One such doctrine of theirs, that may shock you, and it should, is their belief that the doctrine of the trinity is a doctrine of the devil. However they are not alone in this belief because like the Jehovah's Witnesses, United Pentecostals and Adventists also misinterpret the Scriptures concerning the oneness of God. When they agree with the Word of God, then we can agree as well. One area upon which we can agree, is where the Bible teaches that there is one God.

"Hear O Israel, Jehovah, our God is one Jehovah"
(Deuteronomy 6:4)

"Thou believest that God is one; thou doest well; the demons also believe and shudder" (James 2:29)

"And the scribe said unto Him; Well, Master, thou hast said the truth; for there is one God, and there is

45

none other but He" (Mark 12:32)

There are many passages that apprise us of the fact that there is only one God – the Creator of the universe, and the giver of life, on that point we can agree. However, where they and the Word of God disagree, is the idea that *'one'* God means there can only be *'one'* personage in God. The Jehovah's Witnesses argue that to believe there are three personages, means that you must believe in three gods – which is a false supposition. A conclusion cannot be forced into a passage that is not supported by evidence, or context, which is what the Anti-Godhead types have done. The Jehovah's Witnesses have supplied no rational evidence that supports their theory, and that is all it is - a theory.

The Oneness Pentecostals, Adventists and Moslems try desperately to make the same argument, but they all fail. It is agreed that the word *'trinity'* is found nowhere in the Bible; however, that does not mean that the concept is not taught. No where do we find the name *'Jehovah's Witnesses'* in the Bible, yet they teach that the concept is there by taking Scriptures out of context. It is very important that we are extremely careful as to how we reason through the Scriptures; and that we do not take passages out of context in order to force an interpretation. Most arguments made by Jehovah's Witnesses can be used against them, which has been shown to be the case with the name *'Jehovah's Witnesses,'* not being found in the Bible. Concerning their false belief that there is no trinity taught in the Bible, we find the following arguments made by Judge Rutherford:

"The doctrine of the trinity was first introduced into the Christian church by a clergyman of Antioch, named Theophilus. That there are three gods in one; to wit, God the Father, God the Son and God the Holy Spirit, all three equal in power, substance and eternity. Never was there a more deceptive doctrine advanced than that of the trinity, it could have originated only in one mind, and that the mind of Satan the Devil." [39]

"There is but one God, the Creator of heaven and earth, and the giver of life to all creation. Jesus is the Son of God, the beginning of God's creation and great executive officer of God in carrying His plan into operation. The Holy Spirit is the invisible power of God which He gives to, and which is used by, those who are in full harmony with Him." [40]

Again under the heading *"Lies,"* Judge Rutherford states the following:

"The doctrine of the "trinity" finds no support whatsoever in the Bible, but, on the contrary, the Bible proves beyond all doubt that it is the Devil's doctrine, fraudulently imposed upon men to destroy their faith in Jehovah God and His gracious provision for the redemption and regeneration of the human

---

[39] J.F. Rutherford, **Reconciliation** (Watch Tower Bible & Tract Society, 1928) p. 100, 101
[40] Ibid, p. 103

race. Therefore it definitely appears that the doctrine of the so-called "holy trinity" is another of Satan's lies." [41]

It is clear from the writings of Mr. Rutherford, that the Jehovah's Witnesses believe that there is one God, and God is only one person, and that person is God the Father, Jehovah. They also believe that God the Father created Jesus the Son, who in the future would sacrifice His *'Perfect Human Life,'* so that men could regain what they lost in Adam. We learn also from them that God the Father created *"Holy Spirit"* as they refer to Him. Not *'the'* Holy Spirit – just Holy Spirit [see p. 240]. Holy Spirit is an *"it"* according to the Jehovah's Witnesses. [42] They believe He is nothing more than a force, like electricity. This holy force or electricity is used by God the Father (Jehovah) to do whatever needs to be done. There are other religious groups who believe the same thing about the Holy Spirit – Adventists, United Pentecostals, Full Gospel Churches, and others. We will look more into each of these persons of the Godhead as this chapter progresses.

As a side note, there is a very dangerous doctrine being promulgated by the Witnesses. This is the doctrine of Bible misinterpretation, something that regrettably all denominations do, which is why religious division exists. This doctrine promotes the erroneous idea that it doesn't really matter what a person believes, or the notion that one church is

---

[41] J.F. Rutherford, **Riches** (Watch Tower Bible & Tract Society, 1936) p. 188

[42] J.F. Rutherford, **Reconciliation** (Watch Tower Bible & Tract Society, 1928) p. 114

as good as another; concepts that are taught nowhere in the Bible. The Bible doctrine of unity insinuates believing and teaching the **same** doctrine (1 Corinthians 1:10; John 17:20-21; Philippians 3:16). If it were true, that God didn't care what we believe or teach, then the Jehovah's Witnesses and others like them would be correct concerning whatever they choose to believe about the Holy Spirit, Jesus [see p. 242], and the Father, and we should just stop right here and let them go on teaching their doctrine to others. If it doesn't matter to God what is believed or taught, then it would be a sin for any one, including this volume, to expose a doctrine as erroneous, because there would be no such thing.

The truth of the matter is that God has commanded that our beliefs and teachings agree.

> "Now I beseech you, brethren, by the name of the Lord Jesus Christ, that you all **speak the same thing**, and that there be **no divisions** among you; but that you be perfectly joined together in the same mind and in the same judgment" (1 Corinthians 1:10) [Emphasis mine]

> "Nevertheless, whereto we have already attained, let us **walk by the same rule**, let us mind the same thing" (Philippians 3:16) [Emphasis mine]

All men are commanded to teach no other doctrine than what the apostles taught.

"As I besought thee to abide still at Ephesus, when I went into Macedonia, that thou mighest charge some that they __teach no other doctrine__." (1 Timothy 1:3) [Emphasis mine]

All men are to nourish themselves in the words of faith and good doctrine.

"If thou put the brethren in remembrance of these things, thou shalt be a good minister of Jesus Christ, nourished up in the words of faith and of __good doctrine__, whereunto thou hast attained." (1 Timothy 4:6) [Emphasis mine]

Teaching that the doctrine of the *'Trinity'* [see p. 260], is of the devil is erroneous doctrine in and of itself, and blasphemes the Holy Spirit who gave us God's word concerning the Godhead.

"And Jesus answered and said, while He taught in the temple, how say the scribes that Christ is the son of David? For __David himself said by the Holy Spirit__, the Lord said to my Lord, sit thou on my right hand, till I make thine enemies thy footstool. David therefore himself calleth him Lord; and whence is he then his son? And the people heard Him gladly." (Mark 12:35-37) [Emphasis mine]

"Knowing this first, that no prophecy of the Scripture is of any private interpretation. For the prophecy came not in old time by the will of man: but holy men

*of God spake as they were moved by the **Holy Spirit**.*" (2 Peter 1:20-21) [Emphasis mine]

The doctrine of the Witnesses concerning the Godhead is based upon irrational arguments and unsound logic. Many of the arguments used by the Jehovah's Witnesses to defend their beliefs, is because the Roman Catholic Church said it; [43] as if the Catholic Church has any authority for anything. The Catholic Church is just as mistaken in its teachings as are the Jehovah's Witnesses. In their book "*The Truth that Leads to Eternal Life*," written by the Watch Tower Bible and Tract Society, under the heading "*Who is God?*" on page 22, we find this statement concerning the trinity:

> "*Many religions of Christendom teach that God is a "trinity" although the word "trinity" does not appear in the Bible. This doctrine was unknown to the Hebrew prophets and Christian apostles. When Jesus was on earth he certainly was not equal to his Father. As for the Holy Spirit, the so-called third person of the trinity, we have already seen that IT is not a person, but God's active force.*"

Let us examine the assumption made by the Watch Tower concerning the doctrine of the Trinity. According to the Watch Tower Society, the doctrine of the trinity was unknown to the Hebrew prophets and Christian apostles. Where is their proof? They give none! They simply craft a statement, as if that's

---

[43] **Let God be True**, (Watch Tower Bible & Tract Society, 1946) p. 100

enough evidence to make their case, which of course it is for members of the Jehovah's Witnesses, because they must accept without question such doctrine. It matters not, that the Watch Tower does not prove their assumptions; we are simply expected to accept what they say without question, [44] as their members do.

Regrettably, the vast majority of people they study with are unaware of what the Bible teaches on many subjects. They are easily swayed to accept the Witnesses interpretation of Scripture, because they appear to give plausible explanations. Remember, the Witnesses challenge all prospective members to be like the Bereans of Acts 17:11, who challenged Paul and put his doctrine to the test. The hypocrisy of the Witnesses shines through, because anyone deciding to join the ranks of the Witnesses, had better not put them to the test or else he will be kicked out. In fact, he probably won't even become a Witness, because he would no longer be considered a person of 'good will.'

The Hebrews (Israelites) knew perfectly well that there were three distinct personages in one God. The evidence is found in the first chapter of the book of Genesis, written by Moses, who was a Hebrew.

> *"In the beginning God (Elohim) created the heavens and the earth"* (Genesis 1:1)

---

[44] **Organized to Do God's Will**, (Watch Tower Bible and Tract Society, 2005) pp. 20, 146

If Moses knew nothing of the '*Trinity*' then he chose a strange Hebrew word to describe God – '*Elohim*.' Elohim is a plural word, signifying that there was more than one personage at the creation event, and more than one personage in the beginning. But the Jehovah's Witnesses irrationally deny this, as do Pentecostals. The Witnesses argue that Jehovah God was in the beginning, and that He created the Logos who became Jesus Christ in the flesh [see p. 241 – incarnation], and that Jehovah God used His new creation, the Logos, to create the heavens and the earth and everything else in the universe. They assert that the '*Logos*' was not God, but '*a god,*' and that Jehovah used '*a god*' to create all things. [45] Only the irrational minded will deny the plurality of the word '*Elohim*.' [46]

They assert without proof that "*When Jesus was on earth he certainly was not equal to his Father.*" [47] Again, they expect no one to question them, just accept what they say as the truth. Did Jesus, while on earth, equate Himself equal to God the Father? Without a doubt. Why else did the Jews hate Him? Not only did Jesus equate Himself equal to God the Father, but His apostles did as well. When Jesus told the man sick with palsy that his sins were forgiven, the scribes (Hebrews) considered Jesus a blasphemer – why? Because they knew only God could forgive sins and they understood that Jesus was equating Himself equal with God!

---

[45] J.F. Rutherford, **Creation** (Watch Tower Bible & Tract Society, 1928), pp. 11, 12

[46] Merrill C. Tenny, **The Zondervan Pictorial Encyclopedia of the Bible**, (Regency Reference Library, 1975), pp. 294, 295, 763

[47] **Should You Believe in the Trinity?** (Watch Tower Bible & Tract Society, 1989) pp. 6, 13

"When Jesus saw their faith, He said unto the sick of the palsy, Son, thy sins are forgiven thee. But there were certain of the scribes sitting there, and reasoning in their hearts, why doth this man thus speak blasphemies? Who can forgive sins but God only?" (Mark 2:7)

The Messianic prophet Isaiah spoke of Jesus when he foretold:

"I, even I, am He that blotteth out thy transgressions for Mine own sake, and will not remember thy sins" (Isaiah 43:25)

When Jesus spoke of His sheep, He told His disciples that He and the Father were one, the Jews understood exactly what Jesus meant, and took up stones to stone Him for blasphemy.

"But ye believe not, because ye are not of My sheep. My sheep hear My voice, and I know them, and they follow Me: and I give unto them eternal life; and they shall never perish, neither shall any man pluck them out of My hand. My Father, which gave them Me, is greater than all; and no man is able to pluck them out of My Father's hand. I and My Father are one. Then the Jews took up stones to stone Him. Jesus answered them, Many good works have I shewed you from My Father; for which of those works do ye stone Me? The Jews answered Him, saying, for a good work we stone Thee not; but for blasphemy; and because that

Thou, being a man, makest thyself God." (John 10:26-33).

In John 14:6-12, Jesus informed His apostles that He and the Father were a united one, which could only be equated to God. Later, the apostle Paul confirmed the deity of Christ when he wrote that Jesus emptied Himself of His divine estate to become a man and provide salvation for the world.

"Who, existing in the form of God, thought it not robbery to be equal with God: But emptied Himself, and took upon Him the form of a servant, and was made in the likeness of men:" (Philippians 2:6-8)

Even John, the disciple whom Jesus loved, wrote that Jesus was Deity in eternity before He was made flesh and blood. We have inspired confirmation that Jesus was and is Jehovah God. Yet it is a text that the Witnesses have re-written to fit their pre-conceived doctrine.

"In the beginning was the Word, and the Word was with God, and the Word was God. The same was in the beginning with God. All things were made by Him; and without Him was not anything made that was made.....And the Word was made flesh, and dwelt among us, the glory of the only begotten of the Father, full of grace and truth." (John 1:1-3, 14)

In the book of Revelation, once again John establishes the divinity of Christ by calling Him the first and the last, the

Alpha and Omega, Almighty God.

> *"Behold, he cometh with clouds, and every eye shall see Him, and they also which pierced Him: and all kindreds of the earth shall wail because of Him. Even so, Amen. I am Alpha and Omega, the beginning and the ending, saith the Lord, which is, and which was, and which is to come, the Almighty."* (Revelation 1:7-8)

In Chapter Three of Revelation, speaking to the church in Philadelphia, Jesus describes Himself as *"He that is holy and true"* (Revelation 3:7). Scripture apprises us of the fact that God alone is Holy, as holiness resides in God Himself (Psalm 99:5; Leviticus 11:44-45; 1 Samuel 2:2; et al). Another attribute of God is truth (Jeremiah 10:10; John 17:3; 1 Thessalonians 1:9).

> *"Into Thine hand I commit my spirit: Thou hast redeemed me, O Lord God of truth"* (Psalm 31:5)

> *"The Lord liveth, in truth, in judgment, and in righteousness.."* (Jeremiah 4:2)

One of the proofs used by the Witnesses to disprove the trinity is a quote from the Catholic Encyclopedia. [48] Again, who cares what the Roman Catholic Church or their Encyclopedia has to say about anything. They are the invention of men, not God.

---

[48] **Let God be True**, (Watch Tower Bible & Tract Society, 1946), p. 100

Their doctrines are as unbiblical as those of the Watch Tower Society. All we should concern ourselves with is what does the Bible say? Did God reveal in His inspired Word, the concept of the trinity? If not, then the Jehovah's Witnesses should be given an apology. However, if God did reveal the trinity concept in His Word, then the Jehovah's Witnesses need to repent and turn away from their error. The Bible clearly refutes the assumptions made by the Jehovah's Witnesses concerning the Godhead. Jesus, His apostles, as well as the Hebrews, knew and understood that Jesus was and is Jehovah God.

To say that the Hebrews and apostles knew nothing of the trinity is dishonest at best. God inspired the Old and New Testament writers to record His words - words that taught this very doctrine. The reason the Jehovah's Witnesses teach falsely concerning the Godhead is, (1) Their founder Charles Russell misled them; (2) They totally misunderstand God's character and nature, which has caused a multitude of false doctrines to raise their ugly head over the centuries. We are in agreement with a statement made by Mr. Rutherford when he said:

> *"It is impossible to have a correct understanding of the divine plan of reconciliation of man to God until the proper relationship of Jesus and God is understood."* [49]

This is the reason this chapter has been included in this book –

---

[49] J.F. Rutherford, **Reconciliation** (Watch Tower Bible & Tract Society, 1928) p. 102

to show the true relationship of Jesus and God as taught in the Scriptures, not in the way the Watch Tower Society believes it should be. The reason denominational Christianity exists, is because men and women care more about their right to religious freedom and what other men believe and teach, than what God has revealed through His Word. What many fail to understand, is that Scripture employs different names to represent God's nature, and to assist men to better understand the relationship God desires with humanity.

At one time in man's history, names contained meaning behind them. When parents chose a name for their baby, some event in their lives or the recent life of the child, would be embodied in the name that was given. This was true with the names of people in the Bible. We find the name '*Eve*' meaning "*mother of all living*" (Genesis 3:20), or the name given to Noah which meant "*Comforter*" (Genesis 5:20), and then there was the name Moses denoting his being "*saved from the water*" (Exodus 2:10).

When we analyze the names of our Lord and Savior, we learn that Jesus Christ was not His first and last name, but descriptions of who He was in relation to mankind and God.

> "*Thou shalt call His name Jesus, for He shall save His people from their sins*" (Matthew 1:21)

What we find in the text is a Greek transliteration of the Hebrew name Joshua (yeshua/Jeshua) which insinuates, "*Jehovah is deliverance or salvation*" (International Bible

Standard Encyclopedia). Thus in short, the name '*Jesus*' means "*Savior;*" while the designation Christ denotes, "*anointed one.*" From the prophecy of Isaiah we are given the name "*Emmanuel*" signifying "*God with us*" (Isaiah 7:14; Matthew 1:23). Regrettably, the Jehovah's Witnesses think they are clever by rewording this prophecy in their Bible (The New World Translation) as – "*With us is God.*" They assume this solves the problem of Jesus being God on earth. However, in order to them to be consistent, they should have worded it in the same manner as they did John 1:1 in support of their idea that Jesus is a created being and is '*a god;*' but they didn't, and so their translation agrees with all other translations, that Jehovah God is Emmanuel in the flesh.

The Watch Tower Society has allowed their faith in their founder to prevent the Bible from harmonizing itself. They have allowed their founder, who gleaned doctrine from various denominations and secular religions to become their standard bearer, rather than God's word. The doctrine of the trinity as taught in the Scriptures, makes the sacrifice of Jesus extraordinarily glorious. To comprehend that Jehovah God took it upon Himself to live in the flesh - walking in our shoes for just a short period of time, in order that He would better understand the trials we face each and every day, makes New Testament Christianity even more impressive. What better mediator could man possibly have, than Jesus Christ, the God/man – thereby giving God empathy.

But wait! The Jehovah's Witnesses would say NO! Hold on, Jesus is no more God, than He is our mediator. It's true, despite what the Scriptures teach, Jehovah's Witnesses do not believe in the mediatorship of Christ, as taught in Scripture. [50]

> *"How much more shall the blood of Christ, who through the eternal Spirit offered himself without blemish unto God, cleanse your conscience from dead works to serve the living God? And for this cause he is the mediator of a new covenant, that a death having taken place for the redemption of the transgressions that were under the first covenant, they that have been called may receive the promise of the eternal inheritance."* (Hebrews 9:14-15ASV)

> *"To the general assembly and church of the firstborn who are enrolled in heaven, and to God the Judge of all, and to the spirits of just men made perfect, and to Jesus the mediator of a new covenant, and to the blood of sprinkling that speaketh better than (that of) Abel."* (Hebrews 12:23-24ASV)

> *"For there is one God, one mediator also between God and men, (himself) man, Christ Jesus,"* (1 Timothy 2:5ASV)

Black's Law Dictionary defines the word 'mediator' as *"one who interposes between parties at variance for purposes of*

---

[50] **World-Wide Security Under the "Prince of Peace,"** (Watch Tower Bible & Tract Society, 1986), p. 10

reconciling them." [51] As both Jehovah God and man, Jesus is able to provide an objective and unbiased view that satisfies the dispute between God and man. Being superior to angels, only Jesus qualifies for this unique position (Hebrews 2:14-18; Philippians 2:10-11).

Proving further proof for the Deity of Jesus, let's recount Genesis 1:1 where more than one person was present at the creation event; God the Father, God the Son, and God the Holy Spirit. Not separate gods, but distinct personages in one God. Each playing an important role in the creation process. God the Father stood as the grand architect, while God the Word as the contractor, spoke the universe into existence; then God the Holy Spirit as laborer, assisted in the work of creating all things. Unlike the doctrine of the Jehovah's Witnesses, that Jesus and the Holy Spirit are creations of God the Father; Scripture clearly reveals that Jesus and the Holy Spirit are eternal, like the Father.

Further in Genesis chapter one, when God created the man Adam, it is stated by inspiration:

> *"And God (Elohim) said, Let **US** make man in **OUR** image, after **OUR** likeness"* (Genesis 1:26) [Emphasis mine]

Moses' use of the plural Hebrew word '*Elohim*,' "*And Elohim said*," indicates more than the presence of one person, as the

---

[51] **Black's Law Dictionary** (West Publishing Co., 1979, 5th Edition), p. 885

plural pronouns, '*Us*' and '*Our*' prove. Pronouns are used of persons – people, not things. The one God, with three distinct personages, discussed among themselves the creation of man. They created man in their image, after their likeness. What image were we created in you ask? According to the Jehovah's Witnesses we are beings without an eternal soul, just a life producing spirit.

In God's likeness or image, has nothing to do with God's physical likeness because we are told that God is spirit (John 4:24). Yet we are created in God's likeness. Not only do we have a physical side, we also have a spiritual side. We have been given an immortal soul. A soul that will live on after the physical body has ceased to function. It is in that way that we are created in the likeness of God. Unlike the animal kingdom, we have been given the ability to reason, to comprehend, to feel and to choose our destiny. In other words, we have been given intellect, emotion and a will (1 Corinthians 2:1; Daniel 7:15; Luke 1:47). Therefore, in this way we have been created in the image of God. Lastly, and most importantly, we have been created in the image of God in a way that demands accountability to our Creators will. Solomon wrote, *"Rejoice, O young man, in thy youth, and let thy heart cheer thee in the days of thy youth, and walk in the ways of thy heart, and in the sigh of thy eyes; but know thou, that for all these things God will bring thee into judgment"* (Ecclesiastes 11:9). Because God is holy and just, He created us in His image expecting us to be as holy as He is (Matthew 5:48).

Let's go just one step further in our analysis of God's true

62

nature. If it is true, as the Jehovah's Witnesses speculate, that the meaning of God being '*one*' has reference to God the Father being the only personage of God, then the Atheists would be correct. Believing that religion is a mere invention of men to make us feel better about ourselves; and that morality is a mere invention of man, to make our life better on earth. The reason the Jehovah's Witnesses and Pentecostals are incorrect in their understanding of the Scriptures, is because of their failure to understand what the Bible teaches about the attributes of God.

We know that God is a person. Why? Because only persons have the following attributes, (1) Consciousness, (2) Self-awareness, (3) Intelligence, and (4) Emotion. The animal

kingdom has none of these attributes. We also know that God is a self-existent eternal being.

> *"For thus saith the high and lofty One that inhabiteth eternity, whose name is Holy; I dwell in the high and holy place, ..."* (Isaiah 57:15)

> *"Before the mountains were brought forth, or ever Thou hast formed the earth and the world, even from everlasting to everlasting, Thou art God"* (Psalm 90:2)

> *"But Thou, O Lord, shalt endure forever; and Thy remembrance unto all generations"* (Psalm 102:12)

The Bible also tells us that God is "*love.*"

> "*He that loveth not knoweth not God; for God is love*"
> (1 John 4:8)

> "*And we have known and believed the love that God
> hath to us. God is love; and he that dwelleth in love
> dwelleth in God, and God in him*" (1 John 4:16)

Since it is the case that God is an eternal person, as well as a
God of love, who did God love in eternity, before anything was
created? The Jehovah's Witnesses would have to answer that
God loved Himself, to be consistent with their doctrine. Yet,
God has condemned those who love self.

> "*For men shall be lovers of their own selves, covetous,
> boasters, proud, blasphemers, disobedient to parents,
> unthankful, unholy*" (2 Timothy 3:2)

Logically speaking, in order for God to be perfect in all His
attributes, there had to be more than one person in eternity for
God to love, to be righteous and holy with, to be true, just and
unchanging with. Therefore, the eternal nature and attributes
of God prove by themselves that the concept of the trinity is
true and biblical. Someone might say such an argument cannot
stand, because God is also forgiving, merciful, and jealous.
Therefore, since God is perfect who did He forgive, who was
He merciful to and why was He jealous? While it is true that
God has these attributes and more, it is not logical that God
would apply each and every attribute to Himself, since His

righteous and holy nature would not require mercy, forgiveness or grace for Himself. Those characteristics would apply only to mankind.

The Jehovah's Witnesses believe and teach there is '*one*' God, which to them means there is only one person in the Godhead – Jehovah, God the Father. Unlike the United Pentecostal Church that believes God manifests Himself in three different ways at any given time, the Witnesses aver that God the Father (Jehovah) is the one true God who created Jesus Christ as a distinct spirit being who would become the savior of mankind; and that the Holy Spirit is a distinct creation that is nothing more than an impersonal force – like electricity.

The Bible clearly teaches that their doctrine is false. It reveals that God is composed of one eternal spirit being with three distinct personages – not three separate persons or gods, but three distinct personages in one spirit being; each having their own role to play in the creation event as well as our salvation. The Word of God unmistakably and easily explains who God is and what He desires for us. It is up to us to be open and honest with the Scriptures and to accurately interpret them (2 Timothy 2:15).

Summary

The Witnesses believe the doctrine of the Trinity came from the devil. Their error is due to their misunderstanding of God's oneness. They assert that God the Father (Jehovah), created the Logos and name him Michael [see p. 202 & 244]. This archangel, then proceeded to create all that is in the universe. Witnesses also believe that 'holy spirit,' as they refer to Him, is nothing more than Jehovah's force; like electricity.

The Witnesses New World Translation of the Bible finds John 1:1 & 14 stating: *"In the beginning the Word was, and the Word was with God, and the Word was a god......So the Word became flesh and resided among us, and we had a view to his glory, a glory such as belongs to an only-begotten son from a father; and he was full of undeserved kindness and truth."* According to the Witnesses, Jesus is not God incarnate, but Jehovah took the spirit being Michael with the help of His force (holy spirit), and placed it in Mary's womb. When the child was born, he was given his earthly name, Jesus. After dying on the cross, Jesus ceased to exist, so Jehovah cloned him to stay with his disciples 40 days before this clone was annihilated; and at the same time another clone was created who became Michael in heaven, and who has now been given a godlike status.

Questions to Consider

1. List passages that state God is one.

2. Is it true the Hebrews and apostles never knew or spoke about God consisting for more than one person? If not, provide Scriptures that teach they understood the trinity.

3. Do the pronouns "Us" and "Our" provide proof that more than one person is speaking? Provide scriptures that use pronouns thereby proving the trinity.

4. Consider the oneness of God, and how it does not refer to a numerical one, but a united one. Then list passages that show God is a united one.

5. Is it true that the Logos was first called Michael when in Heaven?

Chapter 4

The Nature of Man

"And God said, Let us make man in Our image, after Our likeness.. so God created man in His own image, in the image of God created He him; male and female created He them"
(Genesis 1:26-27)

"What is man, that Thou are mindful of him?" asked the Psalmist in Psalm 8:4. The inspired penman of the New Testament book of Hebrews made reference to this Psalm in his discussion of the great salvation brought about by the Son of God, Jesus Christ (Hebrew 2:6). In this chapter we will focus upon the nature of man, because Jehovah's Witnesses hold a different view regarding our composition. Therefore, we need to establish the very fabric of our nature, so that we may adequately and Scripturally refute the errors believed and taught by the Watch Tower Society.

What are we composed of? Since the majority of people in the world have been exposed to the false doctrine of evolution, which basically teaches we evolved from some primordial goo, advanced to the zoo, and over millions of years turned into you; their understanding of our nature is most certainly skewed. Regrettably, the numbers of individuals who believe we were created in the image of God are dwindling. Would you

68

not prefer to be created in the image of a Supreme intelligent being, rather than to have evolved from non-intelligent rocks and dirt? I, for one, would.

To a degree, the Jehovah's Witnesses maintain the same irrational conclusions about our nature, as do the Atheists, Agnostics, and evolutionists, even though they do not believe in their theories. Like evolutionists, they believe we do not possess a soul. They contend that God [see p. 237], created mankind with the intent of living on earth in an immortal physical body. However, due to Adam's sin, which prevented humanity from living on an eternal paradise earth, God altered His plans so that our mortal bodies would be annihilated at death. Then after the Battle of Armageddon [see p. 227], God would clone us as immortal bodies.

So we ask the question again, *"what is man that God should concern Himself with us?"* To answer that question we could turn to books on philosophy or even to what evolutionists would have us believe. We could even turn to the creed books of the various denominations, even the books of the Watch Tower Society. Instead, let us turn to the book of origins, a book that will help our understanding as to just exactly how we got here, and for what reason we exist; a book that will even give us information about our nature. This book is called *'The Bible.'*

The Bible is one of two sets of revelation our Creator has provided us with so that we may know things that concern mankind. The first revelation (general) is creation itself, which tells us there is something bigger than mankind in the universe, and the second revelation (special) is God's revealed will, one that offers answers to who God is, our purpose for being on earth, and why pain, evil and suffering exists. Certainly our nature is of concern; at least I would hope that it is. In the first book of the Bible entitled '*Genesis*' (Beginnings), we find the following:

> *"And God said; let us make man in our likeness: and let them have dominion over the fish of the sea, and over the fowl of the air, and over the cattle, and over all the earth, and over every creeping thing that creeps upon the earth. So God created man in His own image, in the image of God created He him; male and female created He them"* (Genesis 1:26-27)

Here it is revealed that God formed man from *"the dust of the ground, and breathed into his nostrils the breath of life, and man became a living soul"* (Genesis 2:7). Why does this matter? Because in this study of the Jehovah's Witnesses a very important lesson is learned about this religious group - they do not believe in the immortal '*soul.*' [52] They are akin in belief to the Atheist who believes there is nothing in addition to our physical bodies; when we die, we die - we are just like rover, dead all over. Let's not just make the accusation without proof, let's read from their material to what they believe and teach about the nature of man.

---

[52] **Let God be True** (Watch Tower Bible & Tract Society, 1946), pp. 74, 75

"If man had an immortal soul or were inherently immortal, there could be no such thing as reconciliation. If man were immortal and indestructible, the wicked would not care to be reconciled but would continue wicked forever, and the good would not need to be reconciled. Both doctrines so confuse the minds of honest people that they cannot understand that Jehovah has a plan of reconciliation. Another false doctrine that has grown out of "inherent immortality" is that of eternal torture of the wicked. Of course life must be perpetual in order for torment to be perpetual; hence the two doctrines of the immortality of the soul and eternal torture must stand or fall together." [53]

As with their false doctrine on the trinity, the Jehovah's Witnesses are again misled. To assert an unsupported argument that reconciliation would not be needed if man were immortal [see p. 240], reveals their lack of rationality. Keep in mind that we are dealing with a group that has redefined words such as 'reconciliation,' as meaning *"to gaining back our eternal life on earth, which was lost by Adam,"* which is totally different than what most understand the word to denote. The Biblical concept of reconciliation, has to do with us deciding we want a relationship with God through the salvation of our immortal souls. However, Judge Rutherford argues:

"The doctrine that man has inherent life and that the

---

[53] J.F. Rutherford, **Reconciliation** (Watch Tower Bible & Tract Society, 1928) pp. 75, 76

soul of man is immortal and cannot die is as false as the Devil himself and is the result of Devil's first lie. The doctrine of inherent immortality of souls was the lie told by Satan, to Eve. Every man is 'A' soul, that is to say, a living, breathing creature. He does not possess a soul separate and distinct from his body; but the body of flesh and the breath of living creatures, together constitute the soul. When a man dies he is completely dead and entirely without knowledge or consciousness. He is not conscious anywhere, and therefore the doctrine of purgatory and eternal torment where men are suffering conscious punishment, is completely false, a wicked doctrine promulgated by the devil to deceive men." [54]

First of all, it is agreed that the doctrine of purgatory is a false one. It is taught nowhere in the word of God. In fact, nowhere in the Bible can the concept of purgatory be found. However, it must be said that Mr. Rutherford and the Jehovah's Witnesses find themselves in the same condition as the Catholics who invented purgatory. Both - are following error. Both - are following the will of men, and not the will of God. The Watch Tower Society wrote:

"Scientists and surgeons have come to the conclusion that man is simply a higher form of animal life, having a more complex organism and capable of exercising faculties beyond those of any other forms

---

[54] J.F. Rutherford, **Salvation** (Watch Tower Bible & Tract Society, 1939), p. 36

of animal life. They have not been able to find in man any definite proof of immortality. They cannot find any evidence that indicates man has an immortal soul." 55

Again, an irrational argument as most scientists and surgeons are not concerned with spiritual matters. They too are materialists, just like the Jehovah's Witnesses. They might as well have used the Atheist and Agnostic as their standard for concluding there is no such thing as an immortal soul [see p. 259]. The only reason anyone would use such examples to prove their point, is because they <u>appear</u> to help make their case. The Watch Tower continues:

"The devil is the one that originated the doctrine of the inherent immortality of the soul. This doctrine is the main one that the Devil has used down through the ages to deceive the people and hold them in bondage to religion. In fact, it is the foundation doctrine of all religion. Immortality is a reward for faithfulness; it does not come automatically to persons at birth." 56

Where is their proof, that the devil is responsible for the doctrine concerning the immortality of the soul? [see p. 259] Not one passage of Scripture is given to make their case that the devil has used this doctrine to deceive men and women in

---

55 **Let God be True** (Watch Tower Bible & Tract Society, 1946), p. 66

56 Ibid, pp. 74, 75

every generation - they just contend that such is true without providing any support whatsoever. Even their doctrine that teaches immortality as a reward for faithfulness finds no support in the Word of God. But that does not stop them from further deceit as we find them stating:

> *"The Bible clearly teaches that the dead are unconscious and lifeless in the grave. Note what Ecclesiastes 9:4, 10 says regarding the condition of the dead. "For the living know that they shall die: but the dead know not anything, neither have they any more a reward for the memory of them is forgotten. Whatsoever thy hand findeth to do, do it with thy might; for there is no work, nor device, nor knowledge, nor wisdom in the grave, whither thou goest." This means that the dead cannot do, feel or think anything."* [57]

First of all, that is not what Solomon is stating at all. It is unfortunate that the Watch Tower Society is very superficial in its understanding of the Scriptures. They pick out verses that **appear** – again I say – **appear** to teach that we – our entire being – are just dead in the grave. However, when the complexity of our being is properly understood in light of the Scriptures, the truth is able to set us free from the error made by some, and the confusion vanishes. Solomon understood his nature. He knew that we are both physical as well as spiritual

---

[57] **The Truth that Leads to Eternal Life** (Watch Tower Bible & Tract Society, 1968) pp. 33-39

beings. In fact, in this same verse used by the Watch Tower Society, we find Solomon using the Hebrew word '*Sheol*' which refers to the same place as the Greek word '*Hades*.' Both words refer to the same temporary realm of departed souls. It is a waiting place where all the dead go to await the return of Jesus on Judgment Day. It is the same place Jesus and the thief proceeded to when they died (Luke 23:43).

There is a common belief among denominationalists that '*Hades*' is just a more polite way of saying hell, and that both words refer to the same place, but this is not true. Nor is it true that when a person dies they are sent straight to heaven or hell. Jehovah's Witnesses have accepted this doctrine from denominational teaching, however with a twist. They believe Jesus went straight to heaven when He died and that He was not resurrected. Instead, God created a clone of Him to walk among His disciples for forty days, while the real spirit being Jesus, was in heaven with Jehovah. The duplicity of the Watch Tower Society prompted them to choose English translations that fit their doctrine, rather than making their doctrine agree with Scripture. They refer to the King James Version because it uses the word '*grave*' instead of '*Sheol*;' in the same way they refer to the 1901 American Standard Version because it uses the word '*Jehovah*' where other translations use the word '*Lord*.'

What Solomon said in Ecclesiastes Chapter Nine, is that when we die, when our true selves (our souls) leave our physical bodies (James 2:26), it is removed to the hadean realm where we lose all sense of time (space and time has ceased), and we have no idea what is transpiring in this life (the physical realm). We have no knowledge or wisdom of it; our only concern is where we are at the time – in Hades. This is why we are told that *"one day is with the Lord as a thousand years, and a thousand years as one day"* (2 Peter 3:8), because time means nothing to God - He does not live in the realm of space and time, and neither will we when we die.

Is this not also true when we sleep? We have no concept of time, or the things that are going on around us (no knowledge or wisdom). Does that mean we are dead? That we have ceased to exist? That is absurd, as are their arguments. The depressing conclusion which this false doctrine espouses, is the Jehovah's Witnesses believing we are equal to the animal kingdom. This sounds a lot like evolutionary theory, does it not? Consider what else they have to say:

> *"The apostle Peter quoted from the writings of Moses concerning Jesus, saying, "Indeed, any soul that does not listen to that prophet will be completely destroyed from among the people" (Acts 3:23). Consistent with this basic truth, not once in any of its verses does the bible say that either human or animal souls are immortal. There are however, dozens of Scriptures that show that the soul can die or be killed."* [58]

---

[58] Ibid, p. 37

Because they take a passage completely out of context as well as change and redefine words, it should be no wonder that they continually arrive at the wrong conclusion. Should anyone talk with a Jehovah's Witness they should be aware of how they redefine words and take subjects out of context. Make sure what they say is compared to what your own Bible says, not theirs (New World Translation). It is true, that sometimes the Bible uses the word 'soul' to refer to the entire man, case in point, Genesis 17:14 and Ezekiel 18:20. However, more times than not, the Word of God addresses the distinct entity known as the '*soul*.' Consider if you will the following Scriptures.

> *"He that refuseth correction despiseth **his own soul**; But he that hearkeneth to reproof getteth understanding."* (Proverbs 15:32 ASV) [Emphasis mine]

> *"But Jeremiah said, They shall not deliver thee. Obey, I beseech thee, the voice of Jehovah, in that which I speak unto thee: so it shall be well with thee, and **thy soul** shall live."* (Jeremiah 38:20 ASV) [Emphasis mine]

> *"And be not afraid of them that kill the body, but are not able to kill the soul: but rather fear him who is able to destroy **both soul and body** in hell."* (Matthew 10:28 ASV) [Emphasis mine]

*"But God said unto him, Thou foolish one, this night is **thy soul** required of thee; and the things which thou hast prepared, whose shall they be?"* (Luke 12:20 ASV) [Emphasis mine]

*"Beloved, I beseech you as sojourners and pilgrims, to abstain from fleshly lust, which war against **the soul**;"* (1 Peter 2:11 ASV) [Emphasis mine]

Jehovah's Witnesses will argue that the Bible is speaking of the life force, and not an immortal soul. Such a belief is akin to the force of Star Wars. Remember, Charles Russell studied Hinduism and Buddhism from which the Stars Wars idea of the Force came, so it is very possible that the Jehovah's Witness doctrine of the soul being nothing more than a *'life force'* comes from this pantheistic view. [59] Peter made a distinction between the flesh and the soul, when he spoke of himself leaving his tabernacle (physical body).

"Yea, I think it meet, as long as I am in this tabernacle, to stir you up by putting you in remembrance; knowing that shortly I must put off this my tabernacle, even as our Lord Jesus Christ hath shewed me." (2 Peter 1:13-14)

Notice that Peter referred to himself as something that was

---

[59] http://www.probe.org/site/c.fdKEIMNsEoG/b.4217915/k.7FF6/The_Worldview_of_Star_Wars.htm

distinct from his physical body. Paul also spoke of the outward man and the inward man, two distinct things, when he wrote:

> *"For which cause we faint not, but though our outward man is decaying, yet the inward man is renewed day by day"* (2 Corinthians 4:16)

In other words, the entire man cannot die or decay, only the physical side was designed to do that, because this existence has always been a temporary one. If there is no such thing as an immortal soul, separate and distinct from the physical body, then there are a number of Scriptures such as the ones we have mentioned that make no sense whatsoever, and would call into question the entirety of the Bible. However, it is not the case that the Word of God is causing the confusion, but the doctrines of men and the Watch Tower Society who are doing so (Romans 3:4; 2 Timothy 3:16-17; 2 Peter 1:3).

The Watch Tower Society has also chosen to misinterpret the words '*destroy*' and '*destruction*.' To know with certainty what these words mean you must turn to a Greek & Hebrew dictionary or lexicon. The word '*destroy*' in the context of Acts 3:23 does not mean '*annihilation*' as the Jehovah's Witnesses assert. Rather, it means separation from God. Through the misinterpretation of Scripture they believe our bodies are the soul; and that we and animals are the same – we are just a little smarter than animal's. [60] They believe it is the devil's lie that men believe there is such a thing as an immortal soul

---

[60] **Let God be True** (Watch Tower Bible & Tract Society, 1946), pp. 66-68

within each and every one of us.

The reason Jehovah's Witnesses must believe that there is no immortal soul, is because they do not believe that an eternal hell exists. Nor do they believe that Jesus is God – or that Jesus was immortal until after He ascended into heaven. One lie compounds to cover up a multitude of lies about the nature of man, and the character of God, until the whole house of cards comes tumbling down. This is the problem with false doctrine. When you believe and teach one error, you must continue to invent other errors to preclude inconsistencies. Even then, inconsistencies will eventually raise their ugly head when confronted with the truth.

Do not to allow anyone to insist that the Bible can't be understood, because that is simply not true. The Bible was given to man by God, who desires that we know Him and His will. God's love for man would not allow Him to give us a book that could not be understood without the help of others. While it is true that there are some things in the Bible that are hard to understand (2 Peter 3:16), the things God's requires us to know are easy, and everyone can understand them alike, if they so choose. Like so many denominational groups, the Watch Tower Society must use this line of thinking to set themselves up as the only purveyors of truth, which was also the case with the Gnostics (The all-knowing ones) of the first century. Unfortunately it is the case that the Jehovah's Witnesses, do in fact, have it wrong concerning the doctrine of man's nature. They love to quote Genesis 2:7 which says:

"And the Lord God formed man of the dust of the ground, and breathed into his nostrils the breath of life, and man became a living soul." (Genesis 2:7)

The most common mistake when interpreting the Bible is the failure or refusal to harmonize the Scriptures (2 Timothy 2:15). Meaning, before you arrive at a conclusion, you must search out other texts that speak of the same thing, then put them all together. Draw only such conclusions that are warranted by the evidence. To properly understand our nature, we must look at other verses that speak of our creation, and other verses that speak about the soul. It is agreed that the Bible teaches God created us from the dust of the ground – but why is it agreed? Because God told us so in His Word, not because the Watch Tower Society or Vatican or any other man said so. What the Jehovah's Witnesses and others of their mindset fail to understand is, when the Bible speaks of what dies, it is talking about our flesh, blood, and bone, which is the physical side as Paul told the Corinthians.

"For we know that if the earthly house of our tabernacle is dissolved, we have a building from God, a house not made with hands, eternal in the heavens." (2 Corinthians 5:14)

What is our *'building from God?'* Both Peter and Paul understood our two-sided nature, that on earth we live in this tabernacle (Flesh & bone, the Outward man), with the real us – our immortal souls residing inside (the Inward man, the building from God). Jehovah's Witnesses use verses such as Ezekiel 18:4, 20; Psalm 119:28 and others to try and make their case, but their argument fails. Sometimes the word '*soul*' does refer to the entire person, as in the case of the above passages, but there are plenty of others, which prove that at other times the word '*soul*' denotes the immortal part of man. Remember, to properly interpret the Scriptures, we must first gather all the evidence on a subject before we draw a conclusion as to its meaning. To make the argument that having an immortal soul negates reconciliation or redemption is absurd. It only shows a lack of coherently putting together all passages that speak of the soul before construing a doctrine.

Reconciliation [see p. 251], and redemption is for the real us – our spiritual side – our building from God - not our physical side. Yet it makes sense that the Jehovah's Witnesses would not want an immortal soul since it is the case that they are materialists. They want to inherit this earth in their physical form, which is why they do not desire a spiritual form. Whether they desire their spiritual form or not, they are stuck with it, because God gave it to everyone. Scripture clearly teaches it will be our spiritual side that will live on forever – not our bodies.

Jehovah's Witnesses falsely conclude that someone must inherit the earth forever, so they devised a doctrine that causes God to create clones of all men, so they may inherit the earth. After all, according to their doctrine, we have no soul, only the physical side was meant to be immortal, but Adam's sin destroyed that ability, therefore, our bodies must now be destroyed so that God may clone new bodies that are immortal. To purportedly cover their error, they teach that God maintains a file of us in His memory banks, so that a clone can be created after the Battle of Armageddon. Does that not seem bazaar? This should be our opinion of every false doctrine.

Since Jehovah's Witnesses abhor clergy, please let it be known that I am not clergy, nor do I believe the Bible authorizes clergy to exist. The only way the Roman Catholic Church should be recognized as the Mother church, is that she is the Mother of Apostasy; from which all denominations have followed, including the Jehovah's Witnesses. [61] It is unmistakable that the Jehovah's Witnesses are not the true church of the Bible, because they have accepted and teach many of the same erroneous doctrines of other Protestant denominations. (1) Original Sin, [62] (2) Millennial Kingdom, [63] (3) Armageddon, [64] etc. However, they part ways with their sister denominations by denying the immorality of the soul.

In Matthew 10:28 Jesus warned, *"do not fear those who kill*

---

[61] 2 Thessalonians chapter 2, Revelation chapter 17, verse 1-5 KJV

[62] J.F. Rutherford, **Salvation** (Watch Tower Bible & Tract Society, 1939) p. 169 – and **What Does the Bible Really Teach?** (Watch Tower Bible & Tract Society, 2005), p. 53

[63] Charles T. Russell, **The Divine Plan of the Ages** (The Dawn Bible Students Association, 1916), p. 290

[64] **What Does the Bible Really Teach** (Watch Tower Bible & Tract Society, 2005) p. 82

the body but cannot kill the soul, rather fear Him who can destroy both soul and body in hell." The Witnesses love to quote this verse thinking it makes their case against an immortal soul; but it does not. As with all their doctrine, they fail to properly harmonize the Scriptures, failing to draw only such conclusions as are warranted by the evidence.

According to their way of thinking, Matthew 10:28 is teaching that because man is '*a*' soul and a life force (which is the entire body), then God can completely destroy both; hence their belief in complete non-existence when you die. Notice the hypocrisy of their doctrine. On one hand they say the entire man (body) is '*a*' soul, but then from this one verse they conclude man is both '*a soul*' and '*a body.*' IF that is their argument, then it fails because it can't be both, - the entire man is '*a*' soul, and man is both '*a soul*' and '*a body*' - as the Law of Excluded Middle demands it be one or the other. Either our nature is '*a soul*' or our nature is '*a soul*' and '*a body.*'

Their use of this passage, entertains Jesus using double talk. He speaks of '*the soul*' and '*the body.*' According to the Witnesses, they are one and the same, which causes Jesus to say we should not fear anyone who is able to kill our physical body (soul) but is not able to kill our soul (physical body), instead we should fear Him who can destroy BOTH soul (physical body) and physical body (soul) in hell. The word '*Both*' clarifies that there are two different objects spoken of in the passage, which destroys their doctrine.

84

Now, let's look a little deeper into what Jesus meant in that verse that both body and soul would be destroyed. First of all, the Bible teaches the soul is eternal, meaning it cannot be destroyed in the sense of being obliterated (Ecclesiastes 12:7; Luke 23:46; Acts 7:59; 1 Thessalonians 4:14). Secondly, the Bible teaches the body is temporary and will die and decay (2 Corinthians 5:1-4, 10; Psalm 90:10; 2 Peter 1:13-15; James 2:26). Therefore, this text is speaking of God's judgment upon men. It is teaching that we are not to fear what other men are able to do to us, because on Judgment Day [see p. 243], everyone will be resurrected to face Jesus and answer for the things done in our body. We should therefore fear God who can and will destroy both body and soul in hell, the eternal abode of the souls of the unsaved. Keeping in mind that on Judgment Day, everyone will be resurrected and stand before the Great Judge, Jesus Christ, having been changed in the twinkling of an eye (having put on their spiritual body) (1 Thessalonians 4:13-18; 1 Corinthians 15:46-53).

On Judgment Day, God will judge both our outward man and inward man, because both are accountable for the evil or good we do or have done (2 Corinthians 5:10; Ecclesiastes 11:9; 12:14). The founder, of the Witnesses, Charles T. Russell, as well as their leaders today misunderstand and misinterpret the Scriptures to their detriment. Pertaining to the subjects of hades, hell, and heaven, the soul and spirit as well as destruction and the resurrection the Watch Tower Society and its founders have the Scriptures so twisted to their own destruction they can't make heads or tails out of what the

Scriptures actually teach. What was Paul talking about when he made mention of the outward and inward man?

> *"For which cause we faint not, but though our outward man is decaying, yet the inward man is renewed day by day. For our light affliction, which is but for a moment, worketh for us a far more exceeding and eternal weight of glory; while we look not at the things which are seen, but at the things which are not seen: for the things which are seen are temporal; but the things which are not seen are eternal"* (2 Corinthians 4:16-18)

The outward man refers to the physical body, our earthly tabernacle. It is our temporary side which was never meant to live forever. The inward man denotes the eternal or immortal soul that will live on forever, after our physical bodies cease to function and die. The inward man is not seen, therefore it is eternal. The Jehovah's Witnesses think they will inherit the earth for all eternity because according to their way of thinking, God created the earth with the purpose of existing forever, and since heaven has been closed, then everyone must live somewhere. However, Paul said, *"Flesh and blood CANNOT inherit the kingdom of God"* (1 Corinthians 15:50). The Jehovah's Witnesses would argue that this verse refers to the heavenly realm, and they would be correct. But that does not solve their dilemma, because there is no mention of flesh and blood inheriting an eternal earthly paradise.

What the Witnesses, Oneness Pentecostals, Adventists and others fail to realize is, the transition our nature must make before the eternal, can and will be realized. Paul describes it for us in 1 Corinthians chapter fifteen where he uses the resurrection of the Christ as an illustration, as well as his logical premise to prove the resurrection of the dead. He wrote,

> *"...If there is a natural body, there is also a spiritual body. And so it is written, "The first man Adam became a living being." The last Adam became a life-giving spirit. However, the spiritual is not first, but the natural, and afterward the spiritual. The first man was of the earth, made of dust; the second Man is the Lord of heaven. As was the man of dust, so also are those who are made of dust; and as is the heavenly Man, so also are those who are heavenly. And as we have borne the image of the man of dust, we shall also bear the image of the heavenly Man. Now I say this brethren, that flesh and blood cannot inherit the kingdom of God; nor does corruption inherit incorruption. Behold, I tell you a mystery: We shall not all sleep, but we shall be changed – in a moment, in the twinkling of an eye, at the last trumpet. For the trumpet will sound, and the dead will be raised incorruptible, and we shall be changed. For this corruption must put on incorruption, and this mortal must put on immortality." (1 Corinthians 15:44-53 NKJV)*

Paul is describing how those that sleep (the souls of the dead) are awaiting their transformation to the eternal spirit world. All the dead are now waiting in Hades for the return of Jesus Christ, who will at that time judge all nations of peoples both in Hades, and those still alive on earth at His coming (1 Thessalonians 4:13-18). Our souls having departed our physical bodies at death wait in Hades for the reuniting of soul and spiritual body. However, Paul makes it clear that our natural bodies cannot go into the eternal realm, because they must be changed into a spiritual body. This will occur on Judgment Day, when the souls of all men and women will be joined to their immortal spiritual body. That is clear Bible teaching.

As has been stated numerous times, the Jehovah's Witnesses are materialists, as are Agnostics and Atheists. Their belief system revolves around what they can see, smell, feel, taste and hear. If it doesn't fit in those categories then it doesn't exist. So materialistic are they, that they rewrote Scripture to make it fit into their dogma. While on the cross, Jesus told one of the thieves – *"Verily I say unto thee, Today shalt thou be with Me in paradise"* (Luke 23:43).

The dishonesty of the Jehovah's Witnesses caused them to rewrite that verse to say: *"And He said to him: Truly I tell you today, You will be with Me in Paradise."* Their argument for the different rendering is that the original manuscripts had no punctuations, which all translators have chosen differently. It is true that the manuscripts did not contain punctuations, and that they can and do provide a different meaning to passages, as it does in this case. Keeping the context is a must, when it comes to proper Bible interpretation.

If one chooses to punctuate a passage differently than what has commonly been done, then context (immediate and remote) must confirm the change to be expedient, which it does not in their case. The word *'today,'* sets the focus on Jesus' opening statement, rather than upon the location of the two when they died. Their choice of punctuation does not help support their case, because according to the Witnesses, Jesus is telling the thief, he will be with Jesus when paradise earth is established, which violates the teachings of the Watch Tower Society; who believe Jesus will never be on earth, nor will the majority of Witnesses ever see Him. Only the 144,000 are given the privilege of his presence in heaven.

The Watch Tower Society implies in their booklet called, *"What Does the Bible Really Teach?"* that Jesus was teaching about Paradise on earth after the Battle of Armageddon. [65] Yet, even then they are deceiving their prospects because they believe no one will ever see Jesus accept the 144,000 in heaven. Those on Paradise earth therefore, will never be with Jesus, or see Jesus or Jehovah God. The problem with their doctrine is, being a materialist purports there is no faith, because true faith is the evidence of things NOT SEEN (Hebrews 11:1). What is not seen is eternal, what is seen is temporary (2 Corinthians 4:17-18). Our physical bodies are

---

[65] Ibid, p. 36

seen as is the earth and are therefore temporary. On the other hand our souls are not seen, therefore they are eternal.

The doctrine of the Jehovah's Witnesses is another of Satan's tools to draw men and women away from the truth, so that they will remain his. Do we have a soul? Absolutely! Is our soul eternal? According to God it is. Does the Bible refer to men as 'souls'? Without a doubt! Does that prove that men do not have an eternal soul? Absolutely not! A careful study of the Bible, searching every Scripture that teaches about the soul/spirit, and grasping how some passages are expressed differently than others, will help anyone seeking to understand the truth. Apply a little common sense, and it will be realized that the Jehovah's Witnesses are dead wrong. This will also give an individual the upper hand next time they knock on your door.

Summary

The Jehovah's Witnesses agree with the Agnostics and Atheists that humanity does not possess an immortal soul. The Witnesses are materialists, who desire a physical life on earth forever. They pick out verses from the Bible that speak of the soul referring to the entire person, but leave out verses that prove the soul is also a distinct entity. The Witnesses believe that the doctrine of the immortal soul is just another of Satan's many lies.

Because they do not believe in the immortal soul of man, their doctrine concerning salvation, the ransom and reconciliation is also skewed. They believe these doctrines point not to our eternal spiritual side, but to the physical body inheriting earth, which they contend was always God's plan before Adam interrupted it with his sin.

Questions to Consider

1. Is it true that reconciliation would not be required if we had an immortal soul? If not, provide Scripture to prove so.

2. Are scientists and surgeons the best source for determining mankind's spiritual makeup? Who is?

3. Where did Jesus go when He died, Hell or Hades? Is Hades just a nicer way of saying Hell, or is a place?

4. Since Charles Russell studied Hinduism and Buddhism, what false religious view became part of his dogma?

5. Does the Bible speak of the entire person being 'a' soul? If so, provide Scriptures that prove this to be the case.

6. Does the Bible speak of a separate entity called the soul, that is within every person? If so, provide Scriptures that prove this to be the case.

7. Does the Bible teach that the 'soul' will be annihilated at death? If not, provide Scriptures to show otherwise.

Chapter 5

Heaven & Hell

*"And these shall go away into everlasting punishment: but
the righteous into life everlasting"*
(Matthew 25:46)

Thus far, we have learned that the Jehovah's Witnesses do not
believe our nature is composed of both a spiritual and a
physical side. They argue that our entire being is 'a' soul, and
when we die, we die, meaning we cease to exist, ending up in
the grave and that's it, completely destroyed, annihilated,
absolutely obliterated. Because they maintain this false view of
our nature, they in turn must embrace an erroneous stance
concerning the afterlife [see p. 233 - death]. As with their
abuse of the Scriptures concerning the nature of man and the
trinity, they again show no proper understanding of how to
interpret the Bible concerning the subject of the hereafter.
They have chosen to ignore certain Hebrew and Greek words,
because they do not fall in line with their teachings; and
instead have selected certain English Translations of the Bible
that help make their arguments.

Case in point – using the King James Version as their
evidence, the Jehovah's Witnesses assert that the Hebrew

word 'Sheol' as found in the Old Testament is a reference to Hell (the eternal abode of punishment), simply because the publishers of the KJV chose to insert the 'Hell' in place of 'Sheol.' Then, they assert that the Greek word 'Hades' [see p. 239], as found in the New Testament is also a reference to Hell. Again, because the King James Version is not consistent in its translation of the Hebrew and Greek words 'Sheol' and 'Hades.' We also discover that the King James Version inconsistently inserts the words 'grave' [see p. 238] or 'pit' [see p. 249], where the word 'Sheol' [see p. 253] should be. It is regrettable that the Witnesses chose to heed the words of an English Translation over the Word of God, but that is how false doctrine attempts to disguise itself. The question that should be posed is this, – which is it? Grave, pit or hell? The reason they use all three as meanings for 'Sheol' and 'Hades' is because it fits their man invented doctrine.

Rather than using the Word of God as their standard, the Watch Tower Society has chosen English Translations and Catholic documents as their arguments against the realms of Hell, and Hades. [66] What they fail to realize, is they are only fighting against God, whom they say they serve. A rational and logical argument is not formulated in the way they do so, nor is it the way you properly interpret the Bible. There is nothing at all wrong with English Translations, we need them in order to read God's Word, unless of course, Hebrew and Greek is studied so that the original language can be read. However, ALL, and I mean ALL English Translations have their errors

---

[66] **Let God be True** (Watch Tower Bible & Tract Society, 1946), p. 89

and that includes the beloved King James Version.

Why? Because men are not always honest in the way they translate or revise the Scriptures. All English Translations unfortunately bring denominational error into the mix. The New International Version is probably the most notable of all, as it furthers the false doctrine of Calvinism. Then there is the Scofield Bible, which furthers the false doctrine of Premillennialism. Even the much loved King James Version has its faults, and one of them is being used to further the error of the Jehovah's Witnesses. Because the King James Version purportedly agrees with their version of the afterlife, by inconsistently translating '*Sheol*' with the words '*grave,*' '*pit,*' or '*Hell,*' and '*Hades*' with the word '*Hell;*' The Witnesses believe their case is made. The translators/revisers should have translated the words in the same way every time since it is the case that the Hebrew '*Sheol*' and Greek '*Hades*' both refer to the same place; the temporary realm of departed souls. Consider the following:

> *"And in hell (KJV) (Hades, ASV) he lift up his eyes, being in torment, and seeth Abraham afar off, and Lazarus in his bosom."* (Luke 16:23) [References mine]

> *"He seeing this before spake of the resurrection of the Christ, that His soul was not left in hell (KJV) (Hades, ASV), neither His flesh did see corruption"* (Acts 2:31; Psalm 16:10) [references mine]

"And the sea gave up the dead which were in it; and death and hell (KJV) (Hades, ASV) delivered up the dead which were in them: and they were judged every man according to their works" (Revelation 20:13) [references mine]

"For in death there is no remembrance of thee: in the grave (KJV) (Sheol, ASV) who shall give thee thanks?" (Psalm 6:5) [References mine]

"They shall go down to the bars of the pit (KJV) (Sheol, ASV), when our rest together is once in the dust." (Job 17:16) [References mine]

As is evident from these few passages of Scripture, the KJV Translators chose to use different words for the same location. Hades (NT), and Sheol (OT), is where every person who has ever lived and died is now waiting for the return of Christ on Judgment Day. The word '*Hell*' [see p. 239], is a completely different Greek word – '*Gehenna*' [see p. 236]. There is no Hebrew equivalent. The Greek word comes from the Hebrew '*Valley of Hinnom*' where fires burned continually, day and night for sacrifices to idols. Hell is the opposite eternal realm to Heaven. Therefore Hell is referred to as:

"The eternal fire" (Matthew 18:8)

"The unquenchable fire....Where the worm never dies and the fire is never put out" (Mark 9:43-47)

Therefore, the Jehovah's Witnesses are incorrect concerning Hell, Hades, Sheol, the grave and the pit. Interestingly, they continually state in their material, that we should, *"Stop! Think! Reason!"* It would be helpful if they would heed their own words by doing this very thing. Yet according to Judge Rutherford we are told:

> *"Hell is not a place, it is a condition of death. That is to say, in the condition of death or out of existence"* [67]

In his pathetic misuse of the Scriptures, Mr. Rutherford goes on to say:

> *"Death could not hold Jesus because it was God's will that he should live again. "Whom God hath raised up, having loosed the pains of death; because it was not possible that he should be holden of it" (Acts 2:24). Jesus afterward corroborated Peter's statement saying, "I am he that liveth, and was dead; and, behold I am alive for evermore, Amen: and have the keys of hell and of death." (Revelation 1:18). These words of Jesus prove conclusively that there is no life in hell, because when he was in hell he was dead, and when God brought him forth from hell, he was alive."* [68]

---

[67] J.F. Rutherford, **Reconciliation** (Watch Tower Bible & Tract Society, 1928) p. 296
[68] Ibid, p. 297

Mr. Rutherford's misperception, is generated by his lack of understanding the Greek language. The word *'Hell'* (*Gehenna*) is not found in Revelation 1:18, but rather the Greek word 'Hades' was used by John. Jesus stated that He had the keys of *"Hades and Death,"* not *'Hell and Death.'* Keys are symbolic of authority, meaning that Jesus has authority over Hades and Death. Mr. Rutherford agrees that keys do mean authority, [69] however he states Jesus has authority to bring back into existence those who have died, (have been annihilated), as if anyone goes out of existence in the first place. Paul points out:

> *"Then cometh the end, when He shall have delivered up the kingdom to God, even the Father; when He shall have put down all rule and all authority and power. For He must reign, **TILL** He hath put all enemies under His feet. The last enemy that shall be destroyed is death"* (1 Corinthians 15:24-26) [Emphasis mine]

The Watch Tower Society might understand that the *'death'* Paul is speaking of, is both physical and spiritual if they would just *"Stop! Think! And Reason!"* [70] In Revelation 20:14, John enlightens us to the fact that *"Death and Hades"* will be cast into the lake of fire. Who is going to do the casting? Jesus of course, because He has authority over Death and Hades! To what does the lake of fire refer? Hell – the final and eternal domicile, when Hades and Death are no longer required,

---

[69] Ibid, p. 298
[70] **Let God be True** (Watch Tower Bible & Tract Society, 1946), p. 90

because life on earth will have ceased. The Jehovah's Witnesses teaching of the afterlife is erroneous because they are perplexed concerning the purpose of earth. They refuse to understand why God would create this earth and then destroy it in the end. Rather than properly harmonizing the Scriptures, they run to the thief on the cross to dishonestly demonstrate an eternal earth.

> *"What a marvelous future awaits those who choose to learn about our Grand Creator, Jehovah God, and to serve Him! It was to the coming Paradise on earth that Jesus pointed when he promised the evildoer who died alongside him: "You will be with me in Paradise"* (Luke 23:43). [71]

Not only did Jesus not tell the thief of a future paradise earth, but the Witnesses believe Jesus will never be on earth, which means He lied to the thief. The fact of the matter is, that God is looking for men and women who feel the same about unholiness as He does. He doesn't want mindless robots to follow Him. He wants men and women who choose, on their own, to follow Him. He wants as many men and women as possible, to be with Him eternally. His grace provided humanity with everything it needs to reach the heavenly goal. He gave us intellect, will and emotion, as well as free will, not to mention a planet that meets our every need. God allows trials and tribulations to occur in our lives, to help us realize

---

[71] **What Does the Bible Really Teach?** (Watch Tower Bible & Tract Society, 2005) p. 36

how much we need Him. When the time arrives, that men and women are no longer seeking Him, God will end life on this earth, and neither physical or spiritual death, nor Hades will be required.

That is all that Paul was saying about Jesus in 1 Corinthians chapter fifteen. He was not teaching, that when Jesus died on the cross He ceased to exist, or that there is no such thing as an eternal realm called hell. However, Judge Rutherford continues to say:

> *"The word "soul" is synonymous with the words "man", "creature", "being." Every creature is a soul. NO creature has a soul. The soul Jesus was in hell, that is to say, out of existence, in the condition of death. The body of Jesus God did not permit to corrupt but otherwise disposed of it. The fact that Jesus went to hell is proof that all souls at death go to hell and therefore that the millions of persons who have died are in hell, which is the condition of death. If hell, as the preachers teach, were a place of eternal torment then Jesus could not have been brought out, nor could anyone else be brought out. The fact of being brought out proves that it is not a place wherein such are kept eternally. But when we understand that hell is a condition of death, or absence of life, and that God raised up Jesus, we can see how he can bring back by Jesus all who are in hell. Because he has so promised and has clothed*

Jesus with power and authority to raise up the dead, he will do so (1 Thessalonians 4:14-17; Matthew 28:18). Returning from hell means bringing back from the dead. [72]

Assumptions galore! That is the basis of all Jehovah's Witness doctrine; never proved assumptions that are based upon misunderstandings of Scripture, English Translations, and Catholic documents, but not the Word of God. Let's look at these false assumptions concocted by Mr. Rutherford.

1. *"Hell is not a place but a condition of death."*
    a. The word *'Hell'* comes from the Greek word *"Gehenna"* which is defined in Vine's Dictionary of New Testament words as *"representing the Hebrew Ge-Hinnom* (Valley of Tophet) *and a corresponding Aramaic word."* It is found 12 times in the NT. That God, *"after He hath killed, hath power to cast into Hell,"* is assigned as a reason why He should be feared with the fear that keeps from evil doing (Luke 12:5). Matthew 10:28 declares not the casting in, but the doom which follows, namely, the destruction (not the loss of being, but of well-being) of *"both soul and body."*

        Nowhere in the Bible is the idea taught that *'hell'* is a *'condition'* of death, or that it means

---

[72] J.F. Rutherford, **Reconciliation** (Watch Tower Bible & Tract Society, 1928) p. 298

out of existence. The only reason Mr. Rutherford asserts Jesus going to 'hell' is because he accepts what the King James Version says. If he would have checked the Greek, he would have discovered the word 'Hades' which informs the honest student that Jesus proceeded to the temporary realm of departed spirits, not the eternal realm of the lost; and that is why He was able to come out.

2. *"Hell is synonymous with grave and pit"*
   a. Only synonymous in Mr. Rutherford's eyes because the King James Version is inconsistent with its translation, exchanging either word for the actual Hebrew word *"Sheol"* (Temporary Realm of departed souls).

Mr. Rutherford further argues:

"Following the death of Jesus upon the cross the body was taken down and buried in a sepulchre or grave. For three days Jesus was dead. His being or soul was in hell; that is to say, in the condition of death, out of existence."[73]

Again Judge Rutherford is wrong. Jesus was not in Hell, He was in Hades, Paradise to be exact. In Luke 16:19ff, Jesus gave insight concerning the realm of Hades (Sheol).

---

[73] Ibid, p. 297

"There was a certain rich man, which was clothed in purple and fine linen, and fared sumptuously every day: and there was a certain beggar named Lazarus, which was laid at his gate full of sores, and desiring to be fed with the crumbs which fell from the rich man's table: moreover the dogs came and licked his sores. And it came to pass, that the beggar died, and was carried by angels into Abraham's bosom: the rich man also died, and was buried; and in Hades he lift up his eyes, being in torments, and seeth Abraham afar off, and Lazarus in his bosom. And he cried and said, Father Abraham, have mercy on me, and send Lazarus, that he may dip the tip of his finger in water, and cool my tongue; for I am tormented in this flame. But Abraham said, Son, remember that thou in thy lifetime receivedst thy good things, and likewise Lazarus evil things: but now he is comforted, and thou art tormented. And beside all this, between us and you there is a great gulf fixed: so that they which would pass from hence to you cannot; neither can they pass to us, that would come from thence." (Luke 16:19-26)

Speaking to the Pharisees and His disciples, Jesus illustrated for them, the death of two men and their change in habitation. Both awake in a different place, both are conscious of their surroundings. The rich man finds himself in torment and desires to receive relief from Lazarus who is receiving good things. Jesus informs us that in this realm, there are two distinct sides, one of torment, and one of Paradise, and that there is a great gulf (canyon) between the two that prevents passage from one side to the other. Neither of these men is *'out of existence,'* or annihilated. It is apparent that Abraham, who had been dead for over 1900 years, is still alive and conscious. There is discussion between Abraham who is in Paradise and the rich man who is in torment. Jesus used this illustration to reveal the temporary realm of Hades/Sheol to His listeners. Keep in mind that some Jews believed as the Witnesses do.

Because this text destroys their doctrine, the Jehovah's Witnesses dishonestly argue that this is merely a parable and cannot be trusted as truth. If this is the case, then Jesus is a liar, thereby making Him an imperfect man, who could not be the Savior of the world. If it is true that parables cannot be trusted as true teaching, then it is also true that Paul and Peter lied when they said:

> *"All Scripture is given by inspiration of God, and is profitable for doctrine, for reproof, for correction, for instruction in righteousness: that the man of God may be perfect, thoroughly furnished unto every good work"* (2 Timothy 3:16-17)

> *"According as His divine power hath given unto us all things that pertain unto life and godliness, through the knowledge of Him that has called us to glory and virtue."* (2 Peter 1:3)

Every parable, every illustration used in the Bible, reveal true situations, otherwise they would be pointless. Therefore, this illustration of Jesus proves that the dead continue to live on in a conscious state after the physical body dies and is laid in the grave.

However, Judge Rutherford is not finished; he makes another attempt at making his case by turning to Psalm 16:10. *"For thou wilt not leave my soul in hell; neither wilt thou allow thine Holy One to see corruption."* Again, more assumptions and false conclusions, which the Jehovah's Witnesses and Watch Tower Society are very good at. Notice the following speculations made by Mr. Rutherford:

1. That the soul represents our entire being – that it is not a separate and distinct entity
2. That the words Hell, Hades and Sheol mean grave or non-existence
3. That Jesus went to Hell when He died – (when in fact He went into the realm of departed spirits or souls - Hades/Sheol).
4. That death equals non-existence – obliteration – annihilation
5. That 'resurrection' means cloning an eternal physical body

The proof set forward for their doctrine is absurd, because they only use passages that <u>appear</u> to teach their doctrine – I repeat – <u>appear</u> to teach. Judge Rutherford states:

"Gehenna; means complete destruction from which there is no resurrection." [74]

Who knows where his definition came from, but it is not the accepted definition. The Greek word *'Gehenna'* which has been translated *'Hell'* in our English Bibles, means the eternal realm of doom (Vine's Dictionary of New Testament Words). But the Watch Tower Society says:

"When Jesus said that persons would be thrown into Gehenna for their bad deeds, He did not mean tormented forever, but symbolically for everlasting destruction – non-existence." [75]

Nowhere, is all the Bible is such an idea taught. Remember, we should *"Stop, Think, and Reason,"* before accepting their definition of words. Well accepted sources should be used to properly determine the meaning of words. Jehovah's Witnesses believe that they will inherit a restored earth, and that the grave will be emptied of its non-existent, unconscious dead. Any person with any common sense should be able to see right through such non-sense. On one hand the Witnesses teach *'Hell'* means out of existence, or annihilation, which means *"to reduce to nothing; to destroy the substance or force of;"* but on the other hand they teach *'graves will be emptied of its non-existent dead?'* Since there is nothing in the

---

[74] J.F. Rutherford, **Salvation** (Watch Tower Bible & Tract Society, 1939), p. 266
[75] **The Truth that Leads to Eternal Life** (Watch Tower Bible & Tract Society, 1968) pp. 44, 45

grave but non-existence, what can possibly be resurrected? Actually nothing is resurrected according to the Watch Tower Society, which is another twist in their doctrine. The only beings who will inherit the earth forever will be eternal physical clones.

Neither *'destroy or destruction'* means what they *'assert'* that it means – non-existence, annihilation, obliteration. True, death is the absence of life, that is, the absence of life in the body, not the immortal soul.

> *"For as the body without the spirit is dead, so faith without works is dead also."* (James 2:26)

The words *'destroy and destruction'* never mean extinction, but rather refer to *'ruin, loss or overthrow.'* When the word refers to things, it denotes their ruin; but when it refers to people, it signifies their *'spiritual ruin, loss or overthrow.'* Speaking to the rich, Paul used the word *'destruction.'* [76]

> *"But they that will be rich fall into temptation and a snare, and into many foolish and hurtful lusts, which drown men in **destruction** and perdition."* (1 Timothy 6:9) [Emphasis mine]

Paul is expressing the possible consequences that being rich *'can'* produce, if one is not careful. If fleshly indulgences are

---

[76] **Vine's Expository Dictionary of New Testament Words**, Greek word 'απωλειν' (Thomas Nelson, 1996)

taken to the excess, then it can lead not only to physical ruin, but spiritual ruin as well. Spiritual destruction means being completely cut off from God, with no opportunity to correct it. Which is the torment of eternal Hell, and is why it is referred to as *"weeping and gnashing of teeth"* (Matthew 25:30). Those weeping will realize they had the chance to choose God over the world, but did not take it. Those gnashing their teeth represent the hard- hearted, who continue not to care for the things of God.

When the Bible speaks of sleeping and death, it is using a figure of speech referred to as, *'Euphemism.'* Paul used this figure of speech when he wrote to the Thessalonians.

> *"But I would not have you to be ignorant, brethren, concerning them which are **asleep**, that ye sorrow not, even as others which have no hope."* (1 Thessalonians 4:13-18) [Emphasis mine]

Paul states there were Christian men and women who were *'asleep,'* which is not to be taken literally, yet Jehovah's Witnesses do. When we think of someone sleeping, we understand they are in a state of inactivity that will cease when they awake. This is how it appears when viewing someone in a casket, yet we know the physical body will not awaken, even though the soul has passed into the Hadean realm. The reasoning of the Witnesses, in asserting the literal meaning of being asleep, would require the same logic when Jesus said *"He is the vine and we are His branches"* (John

15:5). Are we literal branches, and is Jesus a literal vine? If not, why not? Of course Jehovah's Witnesses must believe that 'sleeping' is literal because it is tailored to their doctrine. A doctrine that teaches there is no such thing as an immortal soul, therefore when we die; we go into unconscious sleep, which to them means non-existence, where our bodies (souls) are annihilated.

The Witnesses also believe that the 144,000 will receive heavenly glory as spirit beings, while the remaining great multitude of clones will inherit the earth. They contend that the unfaithful will be sent to non-existence forever – wiped from God's memory banks. Listen further to the words of the Watch Tower Society concerning the resurrection.

> *"Those resurrected to life on earth will come forth to the opportunity of gaining eternal life in paradise earth. It will be a time of education for them. "Scrolls" containing instruction from God will be opened and they will need to follow these in making their minds over in harmony with God's will. They will be judged individually according to their deeds; that is, the deeds they do after being resurrected and after learning the contents of the scrolls. By responding to the education provided, even those who were once as dangerous as wild animals will change their ways. ..... God's kingdom by Christ will rule for all eternity. However, by the close of the first 1,000 years it will have accomplished a particular*

purpose toward the earth. It will have removed every trace of unrighteousness. .... Will they be worthy to have God grant them the right to everlasting life? It will be proper that the kingdom subjects be tested as to their devotion to God's righteous rule. Jehovah will give them the opportunity to show their loyalty. How? By releasing Satan and his demons from their condition of restraint in the abyss. By this test each one in God's earthly family may individually have the privilege of giving a personal answer to the challenge made to their heavenly Father by Satan. Those who stay loyal to God will be judged worthy of everlasting life. Any who rebelliously turn against God will be destroyed in the "second death." [77]

This should of course be foreign to anyone who has read and studied their Bible. According to the Jehovah's Witness, death means *'extinction/obliteration, annihilation.'* [78] Death refers to our bodies (souls) turning to nothingness in the grave. Death is simply a *'condition'* where our minds stop functioning and we know nothing; which of course only stands to reason if we are annihilated at death, [79] because there would be nothing left to function, think or reason, as our minds have been obliterated. However, the Bible teaches exactly the opposite. Consider what the apostle John saw under the altar.

---

[77] Ibid, pp. 110-113

[78] **Let God be True** (Watch Tower Bible & Tract Society, 1946) p. 97

[79] The Truth that Leads to Eternal Life (Watch Tower Bible & Tract Society, 1968), p. 40

*"And when he had opened the fifth seal, I SAW under the altar the **<u>SOULS</u>** of them that were slain for the word of God, and for the testimony which they held"* (Revelation 6:9) [Emphasis mine]

*"And I SAW thrones, and they sat upon them, and judgment was given unto them and I saw the **<u>SOULS</u>** of them that were beheaded for the witness of Jesus, and for the word of God,..."* (Revelation 20:4) [Emphasis mine]

Did John see non-existent bodies? NO! He saw *'the souls'* of the individuals who had died for the cause of Christ. Did John see the physical bodies of those who had died for the cause of Christ? NO! He saw their *'souls.'* Did God say He was the God of the living, or the God of the non-existent, annihilated dead?

"But as touching the resurrection of the dead, have ye not read that which was spoken unto you by God, saying, I am the God of Abraham, and the God of Isaac, and the God of Jacob? God is not the God of the dead, but of the living." (Matthew 22:31-32)

In Matthew 17:3 and Mark 9:1-9, at what is commonly referred to as the Mount of Transfiguration - who was it that stood before Jesus, Peter and John? We are told Moses and Elijah - <u>living souls</u> - whose physical bodies had decayed in the grave centuries earlier, stood before them. Individuals, who were alive and conscious, spoke to Jesus. How was that

111

possible, if it is true that we cease to exist when we die? The Witnesses would irrationally argue that God cloned them for this opportunity, as He did Jesus who walked among His disciples after His crucifixion.

Jesus warned of His return and judgment in Matthew chapter twenty-five. He stated in verse 26:

"And these wicked will go away into everlasting punishment"

Russell and his followers would have us believe that Jesus did not mean what He said. Their argument would be that He implied that it was everlasting unconscious sleep. Then to reinforce their doctrine they turn to Luke chapter sixteen, verses nineteen to thirty-one – the rich man and Lazarus. They irrationally argue from this text that it is nothing more than a parable, an illustration that is not speaking of a literal place. They are really saying that Jesus told lies, gave untrue illustrations when He taught. IF parables are untrue, then what else did Jesus tell that was untrue? Can the Bible be trusted at all? Please recognize how false doctrine turns itself against God and His Word. Luke chapter sixteen does not say or even imply that it is a parable. When Jesus told parables, the text says, *"He told the people a parable"* (Matthew 13:33; 21:33; Mark 4:34; Luke 8:4; 12:16; et al), but not so in this case. Even if we were to concede that it is a parable, Jesus never told a parable that wasn't true, or never used subjects in the parable that did not represent real situations the people understood. To argue that Luke Sixteen is a parable and therefore not true, is to be dishonest with the Word of God.

When talking or studying with a Jehovah's Witness, you must bear in mind that their purpose is to divert your attention away from what the text really says, and to get you to accept their version of the Scriptures. The doctrine of the afterlife is only one of a series of doctrines that the Jehovah's Witnesses falsely teach. They use their own Bible (The New World Translation), and their own dictionary to further their false doctrine. They have been indoctrinated into accepting only what the Watch Tower Society wants them to believe. Please know your Bible, study it, and know what it really teaches about the afterlife. Don't allow anyone like the Jehovah's Witnesses to convince you that men do not possess an eternal soul, or that when men die, they are non-existent.

Instead, believe what God has said, that He created mankind in His image, as an eternal spiritual being, with intellect, will and emotions. Understand that His purpose for placing humanity upon the earth is to test us. He doesn't want robots loving and serving Him, He wants those who make the choice to do so. So He built this planet for the purpose of preparing us for eternity, and then left the choice to us - Heaven or Hell forever.

Summary

Because the Witnesses misunderstand the *'soul,'* they also

miscomprehend God's teaching concerning eternity. The Witnesses use the words *'grave, pit, and hell'* to refer to the same thing - death. Since they do not believe in an eternal place of punishment called *'hell,'* they contend that hell is a 'condition' of death.

This condition, they contend, refers to a person/soul ceasing to exist when they die. Their doctrine of annihilation teaches that all *'souls'* are completely destroyed or annihilated at death. God however, retains the memories and essence of each *'soul'* in His memory banks for future cloning at the resurrection.

Questions to Consider

1. To what do the terms 'Sheol' and 'Hades' refer?

2. What are the Greek words for 'Hades' and 'Hell?'

3. Is the word 'soul' synonymous with the word 'man' or 'being'?

4. Does the Bible teach that hell is a condition of death? If not, provide Scripture to disprove such a belief.

5. Does the word 'destroy' mean annihilation? If not, then to what does it refer?

6. Is the illustration given by Jesus concerning Lazarus and the rich man, a lie or based on truth?

Chapter 6

The Kingdom of God

"And he went into the synagogue, and spake boldly for the
space of three months, reasoning and persuading the things
concerning the kingdom of God"
(Acts 19:8)

Jehovah's Witnesses are masters at twisting the Scriptures to build their web of deception. If one does not possess a basic understanding of the Bible, then he will easily fall prey to their deceptive methods. Charles Taze Russell, the founder of this group, studied Presbyterianism, Hinduism, Buddhism, and Pyramidology, before joining the Adventists. It was during this involvement with Adventism that Russell thought he had finally discovered the truth. However, later he broke away from the Adventists due to disagreements on interpretation of the end times. Russell established his own group known as *'The International Bible Students,'* which was modified to *'Jehovah's Witnesses,'* in 1931. Judge Rutherford altered some of the doctrines of Russell, except for their foundational doctrine concerning the kingdom.

Jehovah's Witnesses assemble in buildings which they call – Kingdom Halls. All their doctrines hinge upon the concept of a

115

two-phase kingdom. What do they believe concerning the kingdom of God? It must be understood that when talking with Jehovah's Witnesses, they have redefined Bible words in order to fit their belief system. What many understand concerning the name *'Christ,'* is completely different than what the Witnesses believe and teach. Words, such as ransom, salvation, sin, death, hell, heaven, soul, spirit, the promised seed, contain completely different meanings to the Jehovah's Witnesses. When they identify these subjects in conversation, most may think they believe the same as the Witnesses do; but the truth of the matter is, this is one of their tools of deception. Understanding that aspect of their *'preaching,'* will help you know what you are confronted with, should you try to study with them. They will bring their own Bible, referred to as *'The New World Translation,'* a Bible that has been translated differently – so that it teaches their belief system.

You might talk to them about our need to preach the Christ, and they will agree with you because they believe that is their calling. However, their idea of preaching the Christ is totally different than what the Bible actually teaches. It is hard to tie down exactly what they believe about a subject because there is no one book that outlines specifically what their doctrine is. It requires hours of hard study and reading many books to begin to glean a small understanding of their doctrine.

Again, the core of their doctrine is the kingdom of God. All other doctrines develop from what they believe about the kingdom. Their way of proving to you that their doctrine is correct, is by taking several passages from the Old and New Testaments, and merging them together to make them appear as if they harmonize, as though they are maintaining the context. While there is nothing wrong with combining Old and New Testament passages, sound Bible interpretation does not allow passages to be taken out of context to make a point; which is constantly executed by the Jehovah's Witnesses. If one has ever read their material, a re-occurring theme will be recognized immediately – Paradise Earth [see p. 248]. The Kingdom and Paradise Earth are foundational to their doctrine, because they are one and the same. However, they believe the false notion that God created the earth to last forever. [80]

There is no doubt that the earth was created with a purpose in mind. Jesus is said to have come to *"Seek and save that which is lost"* (Luke 19:10), which most would agree with. Yet the Jehovah's Witness understand this verse differently. They believe what was *'lost'* does not refer to the individual, but to *'Perfect Human Life'* on paradise earth. The Witnesses assert Adam *'lost'* this when he sinned. [81] They believe Jesus' purpose for coming into the world, was to return our ability to live the *'Perfect Human Life'* on paradise earth/kingdom of God. Several of the doctrines Jehovah's Witnesses believe are found in their booklet entitled, *"What Does the Bible Really Teach?"*; doctrines a person must believe should they decide

---

[80] J.F. Rutherford, **Salvation** (Watch Tower Bible & Tract Society, 1939), pp. 358-361

[81] Charles T. Russell, **The Divine Plan of the Ages** (The Dawn Bible Students Association, 1916), p. 173

to become one of Jehovah's Witnesses. Quotes from their booklet will be used to demonstrate their doctrine concerning the kingdom and paradise earth.

"God's purpose for the earth is really wonderful. Jehovah wants the earth to be filled with happy, healthy people. Do you think that Jehovah God's purpose for people to live in an earthly paradise will ever be realized? "I have even spoken it, God declares, I shall do it." Yes, what God purposes, He will surely do!" [82]

No one should ever doubt that God will always do exactly what is in accordance with His eternal purpose. However, His purpose was never to establish paradise on earth for all eternity. Jehovah's Witnesses misquote Psalm 37:29: *"The righteous themselves will possess the earth, and they will reside forever upon it;"* which is typical of the teaching by the Watch Tower Society and Jehovah's Witnesses. The average person who is not familiar with the Scriptures will assume that they are quoting correctly, when the fact is, that most of the time they are simply paraphrasing their version of what they want the passage to teach. The Psalmist said 'land' not 'earth.' There is a difference. The context, which was written by King David, is speaking of the relationship between the Jews and God. God gave the Israelites a 'land,' not the entire earth. But the Witnesses ignore the context and they continue in their

---

[82] **What Does the Bible Really Teach?** (Watch Tower Bible & Tract Society, 2005), p. 27

deception by telling us:

> *"The Bible assures us, there are new heavens and a new earth that we are awaiting according to God's promise, and in these righteousness is to dwell. Sometimes when the Bible speaks of 'the earth' it means the people who live on the earth, so the righteous 'new earth' is a society of people who receive God's approval."* [83]

Please be reminded, that proper Bible interpretation requires maintaining the context, both immediate and remote, as well as gleaning its meaning from the context (*exegesis*) and not reading into it what you want it to say (*eiegesis*). Jehovah's Witnesses are experts at reading into a passage in order to make the text agree with their version of *'religion,'* [see p. 251], which causes them to force interpretations that do not exist. While it may sound good to the untrained ear, which is how they convert people, their Bible interpretation methods are not sound or valid. All arguments must be both sound and valid in order to be true.

Their version of 2 Peter 3:13, finds Peter speaking of a *'new heaven and new earth,'* which they take out of context. The context confirms that the phrase *'new heaven and new earth'* [see p. 246], is not literal but figurative, representing a new order of things. Isaiah used this same phrase (*figure of speech*) to refer to the upcoming Christian age (Isaiah 65:17).

---

[83] Ibid, p. 33

Peter uses the phrase to refer to eternity, after this life has ceased to exist. Earth was never meant to last forever, it does have a purpose however, and that purpose is to give each of us a period of trial that will determine our eternal destiny. It is our choice who we will serve – God or the Devil, and which eternity we will inherit – heaven or hell.

It is also true that <u>sometimes</u> the Bible uses the word '*earth*' to refer to people or society as a whole, in the same way it uses the word '*world*,' as found in the well-known Scripture, *"For God so loved the **world**, that He gave His only begotten Son..."* (John 3:16) (Emphasis mine]. This is merely a figure of speech called '*metonymy*,' where a word is used to represent an entire idea. Take for example when Paul told the Ephesians, *"Ye did not so learn Christ"* (Ephesians 4:20). Paul used the name '*Christ*' to represent the teachings of Christ, not Christ Himself. Yes the word '*earth*' can <u>in some cases</u> refer to the people or to society as a whole. However, in the case before us - 2 Peter 3:13, it does not; which means they forced that interpretation to fit their doctrine.

On page 33, of their booklet, *"What Does the Bible Really Teach,"* the Watch Tower says God's kingdom will usher in an earthly paradise. Let's consider for a moment, chapter eight of the same booklet to see what they aver about God's kingdom.

"God's kingdom is a government established by Jehovah God with a king chosen by God. Who is the king of God's kingdom? Jesus Christ. Jesus as king is

greater than all human rulers and is called "the king of those who rule as kings and lord of those who rule as lords." (1 Timothy 6:15). [84]

A quick note about the quote taken from First Timothy 6:15 and the New World Translation Bible used by the Jehovah's Witnesses. They have a habit of adding to and taking away from the Word of God, which, if memory serves me right, God commanded such should never be done.

> *"Ye shall **NOT** add unto the word which I command you, **neither** shall you diminish ought from it, that ye may keep the commandments of the Lord your God which I command you."* (Deuteronomy 4:2; Joshua 1:7; Revelation 22:18-19). [Emphasis mine]

The text of First Timothy 6:15 actually reads, *"....Who is the blessed and only Potentate, King of kings and Lord of lords;"* Nothing is said about other rulers. Now, continuing from their booklet, they go on to say:

> *"From where will God's kingdom rule? Well, where is Jesus? .... Hence, it will be a heavenly kingdom."* [85]

Although it may appear confusing at first, that on one hand they say the kingdom of God is paradise earth, and now they

---

[84] Ibid, p. 77
[85] Ibid, p. 77

say it is heavenly, when their doctrine is harmonized, it will be discovered that they believe the kingdom is two-fold – both heavenly and earthly. From the writings of Judge Rutherford we find the following:

> "The kingdom of heaven consists of Christ Jesus, the Head of God's capital organization called Zion, together with 144,000 associates, who are designated as kings and priests unto God and Christ. All of such are spirits in the likeness of Christ Jesus. The number will be no more and no less than 144,000 members. The kingdom is the creation of Jehovah God, and he is over all and above all. He is the great and almighty Theocrat. The King, Christ Jesus, will fully and completely carry out Jehovah's purpose. The kingdom or government of peace is THE Theocracy." [86]

If we wanted to get technical, it could be shown that Rutherford's math is wrong, because the number is more than 144,000 - it is 144,001 which is the adding of Jesus and the 144,000 [see p. 260], together which form 'the Christ.' In another book written by Judge Rutherford we find:

> "The words kingdom and government mean the same thing (Matthew 6:10). The governing power will be in heaven, where God's will shall be done; and the operation of the government shall be on earth, where

[86] J.F. Rutherford, **Salvation** (Watch Tower Bible & Tract Society, 1939), p. 107

the will of God will likewise be done. The government must be a reality which will fully and completely establish righteousness amongst men." [87]

According to the Jehovah's Witnesses the two-fold nature of the kingdom will be governed from heaven by Jesus and the 144,000 (144,001) (referred to as *'the Christ'*). Again, in his book entitled *'Prophecy'* we discover the following:

"In the year 1914 God placed his anointed King upon his throne and directed him to begin his rule amongst the enemy (Psalm 2:6; 110:2). Three and one-half years thereafter, to wit, 1918, the Lord came to his temple. At that time he presented himself to his professed people as their King and earth's rightful Governor." [88]

The year 1914 is a very important date to Jehovah's Witnesses, a date they refer to as *'The Lord's Day,'* [89] [see pages 257]. Before anyone is able to become a Jehovah's Witness, a person MUST believe heartily in that date, as well as confess his trust in that date to the eldership. [90] Until they are convinced he believes in the importance of the date 1914, he will not be allowed to become a Jehovah's Witness. Because it is from

---

[87] J.F. Rutherford, **Government** (Watch Tower Bible & Tract Society, 1928), p. 114

[88] J.F. Rutherford, **Prophecy** (Watch Tower Bible & Tract Society, 1929) pp. 104, 105

[89] Ibid, p. 108

[90] **Organized To Do God's Will** (Watch Tower Bible & Tract Society, 2005), pp. 181, 182 [while they do not specially state so in their material, ex-JW's have confirmed this to be the case]

that date that all their prophecies rely. [91] If he refuses to accept or trust in that date, then he might question their teachings, and we can't have anyone questioning what the Watch Tower Society says, because that would be like questioning the Pope! According to Charles Russell, the inventor of the Jehovah's Witness Denomination, the establishment of the kingdom in 1914 was just the spiritual or invisible phase. They assert:

> *"Luke 17:20-31 ... The kingdom of God cometh not with observation [outward manifestation]; neither shall they say, Lo here! Or lo there! For the kingdom of God is [to be] in your midst." In a word, he showed that when his kingdom should come, it would be everywhere present and everywhere powerful, yet nowhere visible. Thus he gave them an idea of the spiritual kingdom which he preached; but they were unprepared and received it not. There was a measure of truth in the Jewish expectation concerning the promised kingdom, which will in due time be realized, as will be shown; but our Lord's reference here is to that spiritual phase of the kingdom, which will be invisible."* [92]

Russell continues to state:

> *"The Church at present, therefore, is not the kingdom*

---

[91] **What Does the Bible Really Teach?** (Watch Tower Bible & Tract Society, 2005), pp. 215-218

[92] Charles T. Russell, **The Divine Plan of the Ages** (The Dawn Bible Students Association, 1916), pp. 276, 277

of God set up in power and glory, but in its incipient, embryo condition." [93]

"When fully set up, the kingdom of God will be of two parts, a spiritual or heavenly phase and an earthly or human phase. The spiritual will always be invisible to men, as those composing it will be of the divine, spiritual nature, which no man has seen nor can see (1 Timothy 6:16; John 1:18); yet its presence and power will be mightily manifested, chiefly through its human representatives, who will constitute the earthly phase of the kingdom of God. Those who constitute the spiritual phase of the kingdom are the overcoming saints of the Gospel Age – The Christ, head and body – glorified. Their resurrection and exaltation to power precedes that of all others, because through this class all others are to be blessed (Hebrews 11:39-40). [94]

Let us carefully dissect what was expressed in the quotes above. First of all, in Luke chapter seventeen, Jesus was demanded by the Pharisees, to expose when the kingdom of God would appear. He reveals that the kingdom of God is not a physical one, as the Jews were used to having under Saul, David and Solomon, but would be a spiritual kingdom. No one would be able to observe it's presence through the five senses. It is agreed that the kingdom of God is a spiritual one;

---

[93] Ibid, p. 284
[94] Ibid, p. 288

however, it is not invisible. The Scriptures clearly teach that Christians are the kingdom of God, which is the church of Christ (Colossians 1:13; Acts 2:38-47). John reveals this very fact when he wrote that Jesus, *"has made us a kingdom and priests unto God His Father..."* (Revelation 1:6). Since Christians are the kingdom of God, then the spiritual kingdom cannot be invisible.

Stop and consider for a moment, what Russell stated concerning the spiritual kingdom. *"The kingdom are the overcoming saints of the Gospel age – The Christ, head and body – glorified."* Did you happen to catch that? The spiritual kingdom consists of 'the Christ!' Keep in mind that Jehovah's Witnesses do not believe Jesus is God, but that He is a created being, just like you and me, as is his brother Lucifer. [95] Jehovah's Witnesses have redefined the name 'Christ' to refer to an organization, not an individual. They will tell you they believe the name 'Christ' means 'the anointed' [see p. 227], however, it is Jesus in addition to the 144,000 Witnesses who are together anointed to become 'the Christ,' head and body. [96] Russell once stated, and which the Jehovah's Witnesses still teach today, that the anointed is a class of people composed of Jesus and the 144,000 faithful Witnesses.

They will tell you that salvation comes through 'the Christ,' but not Jesus; it is through this class of individuals, an organization, which they contend is 'God's government.'

---

[95] J.F. Rutherford, **Creation** (Watch Tower Bible & Tract Society, 1928), pp. 48, 49
[96] Ibid, pp. 196, 197

"Their (that is the 144,000) *resurrection and exaltation to power precedes that of all others, because through this class all others are to be blessed." Theirs is the first resurrection (Revelation 20:5). The great work before this glorious anointed company – the Christ – necessitates their exaltation to the divine nature: no other than divine power could accomplish it. Theirs is a work pertaining not only to this world, but to all things in heaven and in earth – among spiritual as well as among human beings (Matthew 28:18; Colossians 1:20; Ephesians 1:10; Philippians 2:10; 1 Corinthians 6:3).* [97]

The Bible clearly reveals that in the end, Jesus will return the kingdom of God to the Father (1 Corinthians 15:23-26), not the other way around. Let's delve deeper into this false concept of '*the Christ.*' Russell states, "*The kingdom is the overcoming saints of the Gospel age – the Christ, head and body – glorified.*" Notice that '*the Christ*' is made up of the '*head,*' and the '*body;*' the '*head*' referring to Jesus, and the '*body*' referring to the 144,000; listen to their own writings.

"...at the end of the thousand years, the great work of restitution is accomplished by the Christ (in great measure through the agency of these noble human co-workers); when the whole human race (except the incorrigible – Matthew 25:46; Revelation 20:9)

---

[97] Charles T. Russell, **The Divine Plan of the Ages** (The Dawn Bible Students Association, 1916) pp. 288, 289

stands approved, without spot, or wrinkle, or any such thing, in the presence of Jehovah, these who were instrumental in the work will shine among their fellowmen and before God and Christ and the angels, as the stars forever and ever" (Daniel 12:3). [98]

"... Abraham among others – agrees with Stephen's statement that the promise to Abraham has not yet been fulfilled; and he goes further and shows that those earthly promises cannot and will not be fulfilled until the still higher heavenly promises concerning the Christ (head and body) are fulfilled." [99]

Mr. Russell, the founder of the Jehovah's Witnesses, misunderstood the promise to Abraham; because he perceives it through Pre-millennial eyes. He declares that the promise has yet to be fulfilled, however, God said that He fulfilled the promise given to Abraham when the Israelites took Judea with Joshua.

*"And the Lord gave unto Israel **ALL** the land which He sware to give unto their fathers; and they possessed it, and dwelt therein. There failed **NOT OUGHT** of any good thing which the Lord had spoken unto the house of Israel, **ALL** came to pass."*

---

[98] Ibid, p. 291
[99] Ibid, p. 293

(Joshua 21:43-45). [Emphasis mine]

By maintaining the context, both immediate and remote it is untrue to claim that Stephen was declaring the promise to Abraham as not yet fulfilled (Acts 7:1-9). Abraham's promise was two-fold, transpiring physically through the Israelites, and spiritually through Christ (Genesis 12:1-3; 17:6; 18:18; 22:18; Galatians 3:16). So it is false to say that Abraham agrees with the Witnesses, because he most certainly does not. However our main focus is upon '*the Christ*' [see p. 254]. Russell referred to the '*head*' and the '*body*,' of which the body represents the 144,000 specially anointed Jehovah's Witnesses who are composed of those righteous ones from Abel to the apostles, in addition to those alive at the beginning of WWI (1914 – later changed to 1935). Whenever you hear a Jehovah's Witness make reference to '*the Christ*,' you will know what they mean – and it doesn't refer only to the God/man Jesus Christ; but refers to their idea of government, over which Jesus acts as the CEO and the 144,000 the board of directors.

As for the number 144,000 which comes from the book of Revelation, a number that concerns those that were sealed (Revelation 7:4), and those that were redeemed (Revelation 12:1-4); we find a number that is figurative, not literal. The number 144,000 is representative of the total number of redeemed and sealed individuals who lived under both the Old and New Covenants. There is no way of knowing how many redeemed individuals there will be. What we do know, is that

129

this number is no more literal than are the numbers 666, or 1,000. The book of Revelation was written in symbolic apocalyptic language and falls in the same category as the books of Daniel, Ezekiel, Isaiah and Zechariah. Regrettably, the Jehovah's Witnesses find themselves incorrect, because they have misunderstood and mishandled the Scriptures.

Jehovah's Witnesses are materialists, coveting an earthly existence in a cloned immortal body. Rather than accepting the Bibles teachings about the afterlife, they invented doctrines that allow them to hold on to an earthly existence (or so they think). The Witnesses believe God's original intent was for man to live on earth forever, but when Adam sinned, God removed His original intent as punishment. The death of Jesus however, brought back the possibility of regaining life on earth forever. They argue:

> *"While mankind was under the discipline of evil, and unable to understand its necessity, God repeatedly expressed his purpose to restore and bless them through a coming deliverer. But who that deliverer should be was a mystery for four thousand years, and it only began to be clearly revealed after the resurrection of Christ, in the beginning of the Christian or Gospel age. Looking back to the time when life and Edenic happiness were forfeited by our first parents, we see them under the just penalty of sin filled with sorrow, and without a ray of hope, except that drawn from the obscure statement that*

the seed of the woman should bruise the serpent's head. Though in light of subsequent developments this is full of significance to us, to them it was but a faint and glimmering light. Nearly two thousand years rolled by with no evidence of a fulfillment. .... This is the great mystery of God which has been hidden from all previous ages, and is still hidden from all except a special class – the saints, or consecrated believers (144,000). ..Thus the saints of this Gospel age are an anointed company – anointed to be kings and priests unto God (2 Corinthians 1:21; 1 Peter 2:9); and together with Jesus, their chief and Lord, they constitute Jehovah's Anointed – The Christ. ...That the Christ (the Anointed) is 'not one member, but many," just as the human body is one, and has many members, so also is the Anointed – the Christ (1 Corinthians 12:12-28). Jesus is anointed to be the Head or Lord over the Church which is his body (or his bride, as expressed in another figure – Ephesians 5:25-30), and unitedly they constitute the promised "Seed" – the Great Deliverer: (Galatians 3:29). [100]

True, Genesis 3:15 was a prophecy of the 'seed' (Jesus), who would bruise the serpents head (power/authority), and the promise given to Abraham in Genesis 12:1-3 also spoke of the seed to come (Jesus). The Jews thought it was a reference to them blessing the world, but Paul set the record straight when

---

[100] Ibid, pp. 77, 81, 82

he said, *"Now to Abraham and his seed were the promises made. He saith not, and to seeds, as of many; but as of one, and to thy seed, which is Christ"* (Galatians 3:16). In this one verse, Paul destroys the idea that more than one person was involved in blessing the world, whether to the Jews or the Witnesses. Jesus Christ is the only one to which the promise referred. It was not Jesus plus 144,000 others – but Jesus Christ alone.

As a reminder, words that are taken for granted, that possess a particular meaning, are defined completely different among the Jehovah's Witnesses. Take for instance the word *'Blessing.'* To the Jehovah's Witness it means life on earth forever – NOT forgiveness of sins (Acts 3:26). They believe the term 'Little Flock' as found in Luke 12:32, refers to the 144,000 who will be given the kingdom of God in heaven, [101] – rather than Jesus' disciples to whom He was speaking. They believe the *'other sheep'* of John 10:16 is a reference to the great multitude of Witnesses [102] [see p. 238], just as the Mormons believe it is a reference to them, rather than to what Jesus really meant as a reference to the Gentiles.

It is argued that in the year 1914 the kingdom of God began its invisible presence and was given to Jesus by Jehovah God at that time. Much is discussed in their books about WWI being the beginning of the end, and that Jesus foretold this war in

---

[101] Ibid, p. 72

[102] J.F. Rutherford, **Children** (Watch Tower Bible & Tract Society, 1941), p. 188

Matthew chapter twenty-four, even though it is agreed that Matthew chapter twenty-four is discussing the destruction of Jerusalem by the Romans in AD70. [103]

Another term that is abused by the Jehovah's Witnesses is the term, Judgment Day. Keeping in mind that they are not the only ones who misunderstand that term. Many believe there will be more than one Judgment Day, which is absurd since it is not structured in the plural form. The Watch Tower Society believes that '*Judgment Day*' [see p. 243], is a trial period that begins after the Battle of Armageddon and lasts 1,000 years during which '*the Christ*' will reign. Now bear in mind that '*the Christ*,' refers to Jehovah's two-phase kingdom government. It is believed that the Judgment '*Day*' which the Witnesses call a trial period. This trial period takes place over 1,000 years; yet a person is only allowed the first 100 years of the 1,000 year trial period to become perfect, and if not, they are obliterated for good – which they call the 'second death.' Take note of what they say.

> "*Should any one during that age of trial, under its full blaze of light spurn the offered favors, and make no progress toward perfection for a hundred years, he will be reckoned unworthy of life and will be cut off, though at a hundred years he would be in the period of comparative childhood. Thus it is written of that day: As a lad shall one die a hundred years old;*

---

[103] **Your Will be Done on Earth** (Watch Tower Bible & Tract Society, 1958), pp. 264-307

and as a sinner shall be accursed he who dieth at a hundred years old."(Isaiah 65:20) [104]

Russell and the Watch Tower Society since, pull one passage of Scripture out to try and make their point, while ignoring the context. The context of Isaiah chapter sixty-five begins at verse seventeen. Isaiah furnished prophecy concerning the establishment of the church, which is the true kingdom of God, and he employed figurative language to demonstrate that eternal life will be waiting for those who are in the church. The context of the chapter finds the prophet foretelling in verses seventeen to twenty-five, that life on earth will continue as it always has, until the day Jesus returns to Judge the world. Why would anyone want to be part of a religion that has no hope of heaven? Why would anyone want to be part of a religion that holds no hope of ever personally seeing God, or Jesus?

Jesus stated that He would build His church (Matthew 16:18). People in the first century who obeyed God's plan of salvation were added by Him to Christ's church (Acts 2:47). Being added to the church means we are added to the kingdom of God (Colossians 1:13). There are no second chances to get right with God, this life is the only opportunity we are given. Jesus now reigns as King of His kingdom, upon the throne of David at the right hand of God (Acts 2:34; 1 Corinthians 15:25).

---

[104] Charles T. Russell, **The Divine Plan of the Ages** (The Dawn Bible Students Association, 1916) p. 144

Summary

The Jehovah's Witnesses are masters at twisting the Scriptures in order to build their erroneous doctrines. To prove their beliefs, they take passages from the Old and New Testaments, then paraphrase them together to make them appear they are rightly dividing the Word of God. Through this process of interpretation, they assert that God's purpose was to provide an eternal earth upon which humanity would live in paradise. However, Adam sidetracked God's purpose when he sinned, thereby requiring a corresponding price be paid (the perfect human life of Jesus) to get God's purpose back on track.

The Witnesses recognize the kingdom of God in two phases – a spiritual phase (heavenly kingdom) and a physical phase (earthly kingdom). After the Battle of Armageddon, the 144,000 plus Jesus will form 'The Christ' which will bless all those living on paradise earth. Everyone resurrected to life on earth, will face a 1,000 year Day of Judgment in which they will prove their worthiness to receive eternal life in paradise on earth. Those who fail the test after the first one hundred years of 1,000 year Day of Judgment, will be completely destroyed once and for all.

Questions to Consider

1. Is it true that the kingdom of God refers to paradise earth and heaven? If not, then to what does it refer?

2. Was it always God's purpose for mankind to live on earth for eternity? If not, then for what reason did God create the earth?

3. Do the words 'earth' and 'world' always refer to society? If not, then to what do they refer? What figure of speech is often associated with these words?

4. Has the promise given to Abraham been fulfilled? If so, then did Stephen understand this to be the case (Acts 7)?

5. Did the death of Jesus bestow the opportunity for humanity to live on paradise earth forever? If not, then what did His death provide?

Chapter 7

False Prophets

"Behold, you trust in lying words, that cannot profit"
(Jeremiah 7:8)

The Prophesies advocated by the Jehovah's Witnesses, and the Watch Tower Society, are no different than other date setters who fail in foretelling the future. Concerning prophets, God established a standard for them and their prophecies so that all men would be able to distinguish between truth and error.

"If there arise among you a prophet, or a dreamer of dreams, and gives you a sign or a wonder. And the sign or the wonder come to pass, whereof he spake unto you, saying, let us go after other gods, which you have not known, and let us serve them; you shall not hearken unto the words of that prophet, or that dreamer of dreams: for the Lord your God proveth you, to know whether you love the Lord your God with all your heart and with all your soul."
(Deuteronomy 13:1-5)

"The prophet, which shall presume to speak a word in My name, which I have not commanded him to

137

speak, or that shall speak in the name of other gods, even that prophet shall die. And if you say in your heart, how shall we know the word which the Lord has not spoken? When a prophet speaks in the name of the Lord, if the thing follow not, nor come to pass that is the thing which the Lord has not spoken, but the prophet has spoken it presumptuously." (Deuteronomy 18:20-22).

God's standard applies to anyone who would call themselves a prophet, and for the prophecies they would tell. If a prophecy teaches the opposite of God's word, we are instructed not to heed its words. If the prophecy does not occur as the prophet said it would, then we are to mark the prophet as false and are not to listen to him. How many times have we heard men and women say, such and such will happen at this time and it never comes to pass? Yet, men and women continue to listen to them a second, third and fourth time. God said, if it doesn't come true the first time, stop listening to them, they are liars! They are not God's mouthpieces! This is unquestionably true with the Jehovah's Witnesses – their prophet is definitely a prevaricator!

Not one of their Prophesies has ever come true since the Jehovah's Witness religion was first invented in the late 1800's. The Watch Tower Society, which is supposed to be the Jehovah's overseeing organization, claims that they are God's only living prophet. When asking a Jehovah's Witness if this is true, they will answer in one of several ways – *"those prophecies are taken out of context,"* or *"The Watch Tower never makes the claim to be God's prophet,"* or *"The light is getting brighter and we are understanding Bible prophecy better now."* The question is not whether they understand Bible prophecy or not, the question is, why do they claim to make prophecy in the first place; especially prophecies that never occur? The statement that they do not claim to be God's prophet is also false. From the Watch Tower Societies own words we read.

> *"So does Jehovah have a prophet to help them, to warn them of dangers and to declare things to come? These questions can be answered in the affirmative. Who is this prophet? This prophet was not one man, but was a body of men and women. It is the small group of footstep followers of Jesus Christ, known at that time as International Bible Students. Today they are known as Jehovah's Christian Witnesses.. of course, it is easy to say that this group acts as a prophet of God, it is another thing to prove it."* [105]

> *"Jehovah is the grand identifier of his true messengers. He identifies them by making the **messages he delivers through them** come true. Jehovah is also the great exposer of false messengers."* [106] [Emphasis mine]

---

[105] **Watch Tower Magazine** (Watch Tower Bible & Tract Society, April 1, 1972) p. 197
[106] Ibid, May 1, 1997, p. 8

"Those who do not read can hear, for God has on earth today a prophet like organization, just as he did in the days of the early Christian congregation." [107]

"So, does Jehovah have a prophet to help them, to warn them of dangers and to declare things to come? IDENTIFYING THE "PROPHET" These questions can be answered in the affirmative. Who is this prophet? ... This "prophet" was not one man, but was a body of men and women. It was the small group of footstep followers of Jesus Christ, known at that time as International Bible Students. Today they are known as Jehovah's Christian witnesses. ... Of course, it is easy to say that this group acts as a "prophet" of God. It is another thing to prove it. The only way that this can be done is to review the record. Thus this group of anointed followers of Jesus Christ, doing a work in Christendom paralleling Ezekiel's work among the Jews, were manifestly the modern-day Ezekiel, the "prophet" commissioned by Jehovah to declare the good news of God's Messianic kingdom and to give warning to Christendom." [108]

---

[107] **Watch Tower Magazine** (Watch Tower Bible & Tract Society, October 1, 1964) p. 601

[108] **Watch Tower Magazine** (Watch Tower Bible & Tract Society, April 1, 1972) pp. 197-199 'They shall know that a Prophet was among them.'

According to their own writings, they do claim to be God's prophet. Yet, they deny the standard God established for men to know true prophets from false ones.

> *"Some opposers claim that Jehovah's Witnesses are false prophets. These opponents say that dates have been set, but nothing has happened. Again we ask, What is the motive of these critics? ... the need to revise our understanding somewhat does not make us false prophets...."* [109]

This of course is often how false teachers mislead others. They state a truth while it is evident they are the ones violating that truth, then claim to be innocent by-standers. The Watch Tower Society predicted the end of the world would come in the year 1914 [see p. 217], but when that didn't occur, they changed the date to 1925 [see p. 231], and when that didn't happen they claimed they never picked an exact date, and that prophecies can start and end over long periods of time. [110] Not one example from the Scriptures is provided by them to show their claim that prophecies begin and end over long periods of time when the beginning date of the prophecy never came to pass.

The fact is they can't, because true prophecy never occurs in that manner. Because they missed the first date and then the

---

[109] **Watch Tower Magazine** (Watch Tower Bible & Tract Society, March 15, 1986) p. 19

[110] J.F. Rutherford, **Vindication** (Watch Tower Bible & Tract Society, 1931), pp. 338, 339

second, proves according to God's standard, that they are false prophets and should be regarded as teaching false doctrine. There is no Bible support for the idea that God's prophets had to *'revise'* their understanding *'somewhat'* before the true prophecy was made valid. If this were the case, then God would not have established such a strict standard for determining whether or not a person was a true prophet. Remember, God said if a prophecy does not come to pass in the manner or time given, then that is irrefutable evidence that God was not involved.

If you will recall from chapter one, Mr. Russell was a follower of the Adventist preacher Nelson Barbour, who predicted that the end of the world would occur in the year 1914. [111] Barbour also believed and taught that Jesus returned invisibly in the year 1874, and that the rapture would occur in 1878. All of this is detailed in the July 15, 1906 edition of the Watch Tower magazine. However, Russell parted ways with Barbour in 1879, [112] after a disagreement with some of his prophetic assumptions; thereby causing Russell to establish his own prophecies, while continuing to adhere to what he viewed as the most important dates of Barbour - 1874 & 1914.

Remember, it has been noted that the year 1914 is a very important date among the Jehovah's Witnesses, and it is that date to which a person must agree in order to become a

---

[111] **Jehovah's Witnesses – Proclaimers of God's Kingdom** (Watch Tower Bible & Tract Society, 1993), p. 46
[112] Ibid, p. 47

Jehovah's Witness. Russell's timeline for the beginning of the millennial kingdom was as follows:

1799 – The Last Days begin
1874 – Jesus' invisible presence begins
1878 – Jesus became King in heaven
1914 – Beginning of the 1,000 year earthly reign, (The
following changes came later) the start of Jesus'
invisible presence as well as when he became King in
heaven
1925 – The World would come to an end [113]

Of these dates, the only one still retained by the Jehovah's Witnesses is the year 1914. All other dates are not even mentioned because they failed (of course 1914 failed too). In 1943, Judge Rutherford adjusted many of the predictions to the point of eventually dismissing them all together.

> *"A clearer understanding of Biblical chronology was published in 1943, in the book, "The Truth shall Make you Free," and it was then refined the following year in the book "The Kingdom is At Hand," as well as in later publications."* [114]

Notice they admit their predictions continue to be '*Refined.*' If their predictions were truly from God they would not require

---

[113] **Watch Tower Magazine** (Watch Tower Bible & Tract Society, May 15, 1922) p. 147

[114] **Jehovah's Witnesses – Proclaimers of God's Kingdom** (Watch Tower Bible & Tract Society, 1993) p. 133

refining. Most Jehovah's Witnesses today are not taught many of the important dates that led to reason behind the 1914 date - one of those dates is 1799. According to Russell:

> *"The "Time of the end," a period of one hundred and fifteen (115) years, from AD1799 to AD1914 is particularly marked in the Scriptures. "The Day is His preparation" is another name given to the same period."* [115]

Russell accepted this date from the Adventists who believed it marked the end of papal rule. They believe that papal rule began in the year 539AD, and from that date, calculated 1260 years in order to end up with the date 1799. Russell and the Adventists used (or abused) Revelation chapter eleven, verse three as their source for the number 1260.

> *"And I will give unto my two witnesses, and they shall prophesy 1260 days, clothed in sackcloth."* (Revelation 11:3).

While Revelation is prophecy, it is written in figurative language. The 1260 days discussed in that verse equals forty-two (42) months, not years, and even though prophetic days <u>can</u> <u>sometimes</u> represent years; in this case the number represents the same as the '*time, and time and half a time*' spoken by John in Revelation 12:14. These phrases are

---

[115] Charles T. Russell, **Studies in the Scriptures** Vol. 3, **Thy Kingdom Come** (Watch Tower Bible & Tract Society, 1891) p. 23

representative of the entirety of the Christian age, from the first century to the visible return of Jesus Christ to judge the world – of which time no one knows when it will occur; which is why Jesus taught we must be prepared at all times (Matthew 25).

Any Jehovah's Witness or other person for that matter, that does not believe that the year 1914 commenced the end of the world is labeled *'The Antichrist'* [116] [see p. 227]. As for their 539AD date for the beginning of papal rule, it is also false because the Roman Catholic Church and its popes were not established until around 606AD when for the first time the world accepted the idea of a universal bishop for the church. Even then, it only lasted a few years, until the death of Pope Boniface, at which time the world returned to multiple bishops. Not until the tenth century, would Catholicism and papal rule finally gain permanent acceptance. Therefore, the Adventists and Russell's assumptions are based upon false concepts from the onset, which constitutes their false prophecies.

Following, are several examples of the false prophecies given by the Jehovah's Witnesses.

"We may expect 1925 to witness the return of these faithful men of Israel from the condition of death, being resurrected; therefore we may confidently

---

[116] **Watch Tower Magazine** (Watch Tower Bible & Tract Society, July 18, 1985) p. 31

*expect that 1925 will mark the return of Abraham,
Isaac, Jacob and the faithful prophets of old"* [117]

This was predicted *'confidently'* I might add, in 1920, but is a failed prophecy nonetheless. In the 1960's many publications began to point to the year 1975 [see p. 232], as an important year of fulfilment.

> *"This seventh day, God's rest day, has progressed
> nearly 6,000 years, and there is still the 1,000 year
> reign of Christ to go before its end (Revelation 20:3,
> 7). This 7th 1,000 year period of human existence
> could well be likened to a great Sabbath day. In what
> year, then, would the first 6,000 years of man's
> existence and also the first 6,000 years of God's rest
> day come to an end? The year 1975."* [118]

Another prediction that never came to pass, yet, that didn't stop the Watch Tower Society from continuing their predictions. So confident were they of their prognosticating ability they added God's promise to the mix.

> *"The Creator's promise of a new order of lasting
> peace and true security within our generation"* [119]

---

[117] J.F. Rutherford, **Millions Now Living will Never Die** (Watch Tower Bible & Tract Society, 1925) pp. 89, 90

[118] **Awake Magazine** (Watch Tower Bible & Tract Society, Oct. 8, 1966) p. 19

[119] Ibid, Jan. 8, 1975

Remember what God said in Deuteronomy 18:20-21? If a prediction does not occur, then it did not come from God. According to God, the Watch Tower Society does not represent Him. Yet the Watch Tower Society constructed a statement as if it came from God, even though none of their prophecies have ever come true. The word '*generation*,' mentioned in the text above, connotes an entirely different definition, because the Jehovah's Witnesses have their own set of definitions for words. According to the Watch Tower Society, the word '*generation*' always refers to those Jehovah's Witnesses who were alive in 1914. [120]

Up until 1995, that '*generation*' was still being touted as seeing the end of the world appear in their lifetime. The problem they now face due to that belief, is that the majority of that '*generation*' has in fact passed away (gone into the condition of death/non-existence) with only a few still living. Recognizing the futility of maintaining false prophecy concerning this aspect of their doctrine, the Watch Tower Society finally relented. In 2010, they altered their doctrine to teach there is an '*overlapping*' generation, which extends two full lifetimes from 1914, and potentially ends in the year 2114. Notice if you will their change in wording, between an older quote, to a more recent one.

"Most important, this magazine builds confidence in the Creator's promise of a peaceful and secure new

---

[120] **Watch Tower Magazine** (Watch Tower Bible & Tract Society, April 15, 2010) pp. 7-11

world before the generation that saw the events of 1914 pass away." [121]

"Most important, this magazine builds confidence in the Creator's promise of a peaceful and secure world that is about to replace the present wicked, lawless system of things." [122]

It may be wondered why this is important. Because it modifies many of the beliefs they have long held. It alters their understanding of Matthew 25:31-33, where Jesus separates the sheep from the goats; which they believed allegedly began in 1914 with the invisible return of Jesus. However, now they are forced into a future event after their fictitious Battle of Armageddon. Notice their past view.

"Since Christ returned and sat down on His heavenly throne, all humankind has been on judgment. During the present judgment people are being separated as 'goats' to Christ's left hand or as 'sheep' to his right." [123]

In 1995, they revised their view saying....

"Does this parable (referring to Matthew 25) apply

---

[121] **Awake Magazine**, "This Journal published for:" (Watch Tower Bible & Tract Society) p. 4 – pre-1995

[122] Ibid, post-1995

[123] **You Can Live Forever in Paradise Earth** (Watch Tower Bible & Tract Society, 1982) p. 183

when Jesus sat down in kingly power in 1914, as we have long understood? The parable points to the future when the Son of man will come in his glory. He will sit down to judge, understanding the parable of the sheep and goats in this way indicates that the rendering of judgment on the sheep and the goats is future. It will take place after 'the tribulation' mentioned in Matthew 24:29-30 breaks out and the Son of man arrives in his glory." [124]

While it is agreed that the Judgment referred to in Matthew chapter twenty-five is a future one, and is not currently taking place as they have along held, they continue to embrace the millennial doctrine of a yet future tribulation period, which is false. One of the doctrines of the Jehovah's Witnesses that has been discussed in several chapters is that of the 144,000; also called the little flock. Failing prophecy, after failing prophecy, has required the Watch Tower Society to continually modify its dates to fit current generations. Mr. Russell originally set the date of the 'sealing' of the 144,000 at 1878. [125] Then he modified it to 1881, which was then changed to 1910, and finally at the year 1914. However, when Judge Rutherford became President of the Society, he altered the date so that it would occur in 1925, then again in 1931 and finally in 1935. [126]

---

[124] **Watch Tower Magazine** (Watch Tower Bible & Tract Society, Oct. 15, 1995) pp. 22, 23

[125] Charles T. Russell, **Millennial Dawn: The Time is At Hand,** (Watch Tower Bible & Tract Society, 1889) pp. 235, 367

[126] **Paradise Lost, Paradise Regained** (Watch Tower Bible & Tract Society, 1958) p. 232

Appearing in a 1933 edition of the Watch Tower magazine Jehovah's Witnesses tried to show their reasoning for the 1931 date. According to the Watch Tower this sealing of the 144,000 implies the complete number of 144,000 had been filled, it was sealed, and no one else could become a member of the anointed class. As their proof text, they abused a parable of Jesus as found in Matthew 20:1-16. Nowhere in the text, is the number twelve discovered, they just assume it exists, that is, they force the interpretation. In verse 16 of that text it reads, *"Many are called but few are chosen."* The Watch Tower however, argues that the word *'few'* is a reference to the 144,000. They assert (without proof) that the parable relates to the twelve years from 1919 to 1931 which is the predicted date of the sealing. Yet, they provide no backing for the 1919 date.

In 1966 the Watch Tower began teaching that the sealing occurred in 1935 with no reason whatsoever for the change from 1931. Remember, the Watch Tower Society is only composed of men from the anointed class, the little flock, the 144,000, who will be the body of *'the Christ,'* co-workers with Jesus. [127] This group of 144,000 must have witnessed the invisible appearing of Jesus in 1914 to be enrolled in that class. How anyone can possibly witness something invisible is absurd. [one quick note, the 144,000 is also made up of faithful 'Witnesses' from Abel through the apostles, so how could they have witnessed the invisible appearing of Jesus if

---

[127] J.F. Rutherford, **Creation** (Watch Tower Bible & Tract Society, 1927), p. 319

they were in the condition of death, non-existence?]. In 2007 the Watch Tower admitted that their 1935 date was also wrong when they wrote:

> *"Thus it appears that we cannot set a specific date for when the calling of Christians to the heavenly hope ends."* [128]

It's about time they admitted there are things they cannot foretell. If they would only admit they are not prophets of God, that would be a good start toward the truth. Concerning the Battle of Armageddon, the Jehovah's Witnesses believed it had to occur before the end of the 20th century, since they missed the 1914 date.

> *"And if the wicked system of this world survived until the turn of the century, which is highly improbable, in view of the world trends and the fulfillment of Bible prophecy, there would still be survivors of the WWI generation."* [129]

Yes, World War I (WWI) is spoken of copiously in Watch Tower material because it is believed that Jesus foretold of this war in Matthew chapter twenty-four; which is why the date 1914 is so important to them.

> *"It was in 1914 that the 'period of waiting' came to an*

---

[128] Ibid, May 1, 2007, p. 31
[129] Ibid, Oct. 15, 1980, p. 31

end (Psalm 110:1; Hebrews 10:13). That marked the time of the end of Satan's rule, and from that time forward he would not be permitted to go on without hindrance. It was then that the World War began, which marked the fulfillment of the prophecy concerning the Lord's presence and the end of the world (Matthew 24:7-10). It was then that the war in heaven began, resulting in the ousting of Satan from heaven (Revelation 12:7-9). But the true followers of Christ Jesus could not and did not see the 'sign in heaven' until after 1918, because it was in 1918 that the Lord came into his temple and began to give to the temple class greater light upon God's Word (Revelation 11:19). [130]

"What shall be the sign of thy coming, and of the end of the world [that is, the end of Satan's uninterrupted rule]?" (Matthew 24:3). In response to that question Jesus said that the first evidence discernable by men would be the world war, in which nation would rise up against nation, and kingdom against kingdom. That came to pass in A.D. 1914. Jesus said that the war would be quickly followed by famine and pestilence and earthquakes; and everyone knows that these things did quickly follow the World War." [131]

To the Jehovah's Witnesses World War I was the beginning of

---

[130] J.F. Rutherford, **Prophecy** (Watch Tower Bible & Tract Society, 1929) p. 82

[131] J.F. Rutherford, **Salvation** (Watch Tower Bible & Tract Society, 1939) p. 20

the end of things. When Jesus stated in Matthew chapter twenty-four that '*this generation*' shall not pass <u>till</u> all these things are fulfilled, Russell applied that meaning to the end of the world occurring before the last of the WWI generation died. The Witnesses are not alone in their misinterpretation of Scripture. Many in the denominational world have not been taught how to properly interpret the Scriptures. Pentecostals erroneously apply to themselves the word '*you*' in reference to the baptism of the Holy Spirit and gifts, when in fact it should be kept in context as to who is being spoken to in the first century. The same is true of Matthew chapter twenty-four when Jesus spoke of "*this generation.*" He was not referring to us in the Twenty-First century, but to those living in the First Century. The Witnesses believe that the 144,000 must be sealed so that the Battle of Armageddon can arrive, and the Battle of Armageddon must arrive, so the non-existent dead can be cloned in order to have a second chance at obtaining a perfect human life on paradise earth.

Each of their doctrines, depend completely upon fulfillment in the last century, because according to the Watch Tower Society, it was during the 20th Century that God established His invisible kingdom, and set Jesus up as king. It was in the 20th Century that He sealed the 144,000, and it would be during this same time period that the great crowd, which are the average Jehovah's Witnesses, were to be tried while they struggled to convert '*good willed*' men and women. It was during the 20th Century that the Battle of Armageddon would appear and the 1,000 year trial period would begin – yet

NONE OF IT TRANSPIRED as they confidently predicted it would! Now, they have changed their material to assert differently. Instead of stating "*In our 20th Century,*" their material now says, "*In our day.*" [132]

> "*Down through the centuries since Jesus' day, so many unfulfilled predictions have been made that many no longer take them seriously. Undeterred by previous failures, some seem to have been spurred on by the approach of the year 2000 and have made further predictions of the end of the world. The flood of false alarms is unfortunate. They are like the wolf cries of the shepherd boy, people soon dismiss them, and when the true warning comes, it too is ignored.*" [133]

The Watch Tower Society views itself as the champion of God in restoring God's rightful place in men's hearts. [134] After 100 years they are beginning to understand that they cannot predict anything – no one can. Yet, they haven't given up; they are still trying to establish dates for the end. However, their dates are imprecise. Remember what the Watch Tower said about false messengers?

> "*Jehovah is the grand identifier of his true messengers. He identifies them by making the*

---

[132] **Watch Tower Magazine** (Watch Tower Bible & Tract Society, January 1. 1989) p. 12 – Bound volume and CD library was changed to say "In our day."

[133] **Awake Magazine** (Watch Tower Bible & Tract Society, March 22, 1993) pp. 3, 4

[134] Ibid, Jan. 8, 1970

messages he delivers through them come true. *Jehovah is also the great exposer of false messengers."* [135] [Emphasis mine]

Since it is the case that we are now living in the 21st Century, much of the foundational doctrine of the Watch Tower Society has been destroyed. Yet, that has not stopped them from regrouping and maintaining the status quo. Though it is true that the 1914 generation did not see Armageddon before the end of the 20th Century as <u>confidently</u> predicted; they have now decided it would be best to redefine the word '*generation.*' As the Watchtower calls it – '*they have improved their understanding since 1995,*' and now describe their updated understanding in this manner.

> *"There is a tendency for imperfect humans to want to be specific about the date when the end will come. Recall that even the apostles sought more specifics, asking: "Lord are you restoring the kingdom to Israel at this time? (Acts 1:6). With similar sincere intentions, God's servants in modern times have tried to derive from what Jesus said about "generation' some clear time element calculated from 1914."* [136]

Please re-read what they wrote, and consider whether or not there could be anything wrong with that statement? The Watch Tower made the claim that they are composed of

---

[135] **Watch Tower Magazine** (Watch Tower Bible & Tract Society, May 1. 1997) p. 8

[136] Ibid, June 1, 1997, p. 28

'imperfect humans;' yet they constantly make the allegation they are God's spokesman, God's prophet. Yes, even the prophets of old were imperfect, but that did not prevent them from accurately expounding God's word. To claim they are God's prophet and when they're predictions do not occur, claim to be imperfect humans, is dishonest. If they are truly God's prophet, then their predictions would come true, because it would be God who gave them. Secondly, they compared themselves to the apostles, which is also deceiving, because the apostles only asked Jesus a question; they did not make unsubstantiated predictions like the Watch Tower has done over and over again. Yet, they continue to refer to themselves as God's servants.

God's true servant would never make untrue claims, as the Watch Tower Society does. Therefore, they cannot possibly be God's servant let alone His representative. It was God who gave the standard that if a prophet's predictions did not come to pass, then that prophet was speaking for himself, not for God. Observe the evidence for yourself, evidence that demonstrates not one of the predictions made by the Jehovah's Witnesses has transpired, which confirms they are serving themselves and not God.

Summary

All date setters fail in their predictions, and the Watch Tower Society is no different. Not one of their prophecies has ever come true. But that has not stopped them from predicting the end of the world. They use 'new *light*' as a ruse to cover up their inadequacy in telling the future.

They claim the Watch Tower Society is God's organization used to reveal His will to the Witnesses. The year 1914 is said to have commenced the end of the world, and anyone refusing to accept that belief, is labeled 'The Antichrist.'

In 1920 they confidently predicted that 1925 would see the return of the faithful men of Israel, but if failed. In the 1960's they confidently predicted 1975 would see the fulfillment of the end of the world, but it failed. In the 1980's again they predicted 1995 would be the year that the Battle of Armageddon would come – it too failed. However, it is not the fault of the Watch Tower Society, it is the fault of the Witnesses who have been over zealous in telling others about these dates.

Questions to Consider

1. Did God establish a standard so that men could determine if a prophet was sent from God?

2. Did Jesus wait until 1914 to establish His kingdom? If not, when was His kingdom established?

3. What is the kingdom of God? Provide Scripture for your answer.

4. Is the book of Revelation written literally or in figurative language?

5. What is apocalyptic language and are there other examples of it in the Bible? If so, list the other books that use the same language.

6. Is the Watch Tower Society God's power to save? If not, what is?

Chapter 8

The Ransom & Reconciliation

"For if, when we were enemies, we were reconciled to God by the death of His Son, much more, being reconciled, we shall be saved by His life. And not only so, but we also joy in god through our Lord Jesus Christ, by whom we have now received reconciliation."
(Romans 5:10-11)

"For the Son of man also came not to be ministered unto, but to minister, and to give His life a ransom for many" (Mark 10:45).

The doctrine of the ransom and reconciliation as taught and believed by the Watch Tower Society is far-removed from what the Scriptures actually teach, which is due to their misinterpretation of God's Word. Since they incorrectly interpret the Scriptures concerning the issues of the Godhead, the kingdom of God, and salvation [see pp. 189 & 253], their view of the ransom [see p. 250], and reconciliation [see p. 251], is also inaccurate. When confronted with their own doctrine, they will often answer that they no longer believe that particular topic. However, they must be pressed by asking them, if they no longer believe a particular doctrine, why does their material still teach it? Of course the individual must be prepared to provide them with their material that teaches whatever it is they claim, to no longer believe. That's not being unkind, it's obeying God's commands to put all doctrine to the test (1 John 4:1), as well as exposing it (Ephesians 5:11).

The focus of this chapter will concern their doctrine of the ransom, which will then be tied into their doctrine of reconciliation. Understanding various terms used by the Witnesses is sometimes difficult at best, because their material is at times cryptic to the outsider, and is meant to draw them in. There are some beliefs that the individual will not be taught until after it is evident he has put his complete trust in the teachings of the Watch Tower. The fundamental topic concerning their doctrine of salvation and the ransom is 'the Perfect Human Life.' Note what they say about this:

"When he created Adam, Jehovah gave him something truly precious – 'perfect human life.' When Adam disobeyed God and was condemned to death, he paid a very high price. His sin cost him his – 'perfect human life.' Since a 'perfect human life' was lost, no imperfect human life could ever buy it back." Another 'perfect human life' was the corresponding <u>ransom</u> *that was required. How did Jehovah provide the* <u>ransom</u>*? He sent one of His perfect spirit sons to the earth... the one most precious to Him, His only-begotten Son. Jesus thus sacrificed His 'perfect human life' once for all time*

160

... as a <u>ransom</u> in exchange for Adam's offspring."[137]
[Emphasis mine]

Notice, if you will, how they assert without Bible proof, that Adam was given a *'Perfect Human Life,'* but lost it when he sinned. It is true that when God created the universe with man in it, He saw that it was all *'good'* (Genesis 1:4, 10, 12, 18, 21, 25, 31); meaning that no corruption existed in the world. Yes, Adam and Eve were *'perfect'* (sinless) until the day they broke God's law (Genesis 3:6-19). However, the context does not teach the beliefs of the Witnesses. They stress that the only way for us to regain a *'Perfect Human Life'* which was lost in Adam, was for one of Jehovah's spirit sons to exchange his *'Perfect Human Life'* for ours. What is not specifically stated in their material, but becomes evident with careful study, is that salvation is not given to everyone equally, but occurs in gradual steps, referred to as *'due time,'* [see page 234]. For the 144,000, their *'due time'* appeared in the year 1914, and will continue until the Battle of Armageddon occurs (which it never will). Only the church – the 144,000, now receive the benefits of Jesus' ransom, because only this group of Witnesses is now on trial. [138]

Jesus, the Witnesses allege, only paid the ransom, that is, opened the way for a *'chance'* for everlasting life. The ransom

---

[137] **What Does the Bible Really Teach?** (Watch Tower Bible & Tract Society, 2005), pp. 48-51

[138] Charles T. Russell, **The Divine Plan of the Ages** (The Dawn Bible Students Association, 1916), pp. 152-153

did not excuse sin in anyone, nor did it turn sinners into saints, but merely released the sinner from the first condemnation – the condition of death. [139] Note again what they say about the ransom of Jesus.

> *"The ransom for all given by the man Jesus Christ does not give or guarantee everlasting life or blessing to any man; but it does guarantee to every man another opportunity or trial for life everlasting."* [140]

Like all Calvinists, the Witnesses believe humanity has inherited the sin of Adam, which is nowhere taught in God's Word. Only the consequences of his sin were brought into the world (pain, evil, suffering, sin), but we remain free-moral agents, with the ability to choose right or wrong (Ezekiel 18:20-21; Matthew 18:3). The Watch Tower Society teaches that Jesus was a mere spokesman for Jehovah, a created spirit being, who God caused to become a man. At the age of thirty years, and by his symbolic immersion, Jesus became a perfect man who then possessed all the requirements necessary to furnish the purchase price for sinful humanity. Give attention to their words.

> *"From the beginning, it clearly appears, it was agree between the Father and the Son that Jesus should become a man, suffer contradiction and indignities and reproach upon his name, prove his integrity*

---

[139] Ibid, pp. 150-152
[140] Ibid, p. 150

toward God, die as a sinner, and, proving his faithfulness, then be resurrected out of death and take life again, which would mean that by his death Jesus did not forfeit his life or the right thereto, as Adam had forfeited life. Jesus laid down his life and received life again in full accord with the commandment he had received from Jehovah God, and which commandment Jesus fully agreed to obey. Carrying out that agreement, God raised Jesus out of death and gave him life as a spirit." [141]

According to the Watch Tower, the ransom was a mere asset, received by Jehovah God on behalf of sinful men. It did not remit sin, but negated the inherited sin of Adam, thereafter causing everyone to be responsible only for the sins they commit, which, according to the Witnesses, refers to the sins of the flesh, plus disobeying the dictates of the Watch Tower Society. These sins must we worked off through constant preaching, constant Watch Tower study, faith in the ransom of Christ, attending the annual Lord's Evening Meal, plus the 1,000 year trial. There is no salvation for the Witness in this life.

Since the 144,000 now face their '*due time,*' the rest of humanity, plus the Great Crowd class of Witnesses, will face their '*due time,*' after the Battle of Armageddon, and during their millennial trial period. Although the 144,000 gain instantaneous perfection, the rest gradually gain their perfect

---

[141] J.F. Rutherford, **Salvation** (Watch Tower Bible & Tract Society, 1939) p172

human life over the millennium. [142] Because the ransom pertains only to the 144,000 at this time, with the reminder of Witnesses gaining access to the ransom only during the millennial kingdom period (*their due time*); the subject of reconciliation will now be studied to disclose how the ransom ties in.

There are a number of terms that must be considered when studying the Witnesses doctrine of reconciliation, as well as the ransom – terms such as; the body of Christ, the church, new creatures, ambassadors, anointed ones, true Christians, et al. The average person would agree that these expressions relate to Christians. However, the Witnesses use these terms to refer only to the 144,000, not all Witnesses.

The ransom of Jesus, they believe, was provided first to the *'little flock,'* [see p. 243], because it is their *'due time.'* In the future, the great crowd of Witnesses, and all others who pass the 1,000 year test will benefit from the ransom. Therefore, everyone other than the 144,000, will benefit from Jesus' ransom in a potential sense, not in a real sense. This is also true of reconciliation. The 144,000 alone, have been anointed by God to do His work, to be His ministers and to teach God's will to all others (the great crowd of Witnesses). Through the ransom of Jesus, the 144,000 have been reconciled to God in order that He could give them the *'ministry of reconciliation'* (2 Corinthians 5:17-19). From these words of Paul, the

---

[142] Charles T. Russell, **The Divine Plan of the Ages** (The Dawn Bible Students Association, 1916) p. 153

Witnesses assert that *'the Christ'* (Jesus plus the 144,000), who is also referred to as God's organization, will reconcile the world to God. [143]

In examination of what Paul said in 2 Corinthians 5:17-20, concerning the *'ministry of reconciliation,'* we must view the context, which is something the Witnesses always fail to do. Paul wrote:

> *"Therefore if any man be in Christ, he is a new creature: old things are passed away; behold, all things are become new. And all things are of God, who hath reconciled us to Himself through Jesus Christ, and hath given to us the ministry of reconciliation; to wit, that God was in Christ, reconciling the world unto Himself, not imputing their trespasses unto them; and hath committed unto us the word of reconciliation. Now then we are ambassadors for Christ, as though God did beseech you by us: we pray you in Christ's stead, be ye reconciled to God."*

The context apprises us that Paul is writing to Christians living in the city of Corinth. As one of the apostles, Paul is reminding the Corinthians that God gave the apostles the *'ministry of reconciliation,'* – this ministry was the preaching of the gospel, which is God's power to save or to reconcile (Romans

---

[143] J.F. Rutherford, **Reconciliation** (Watch Tower Bible & Tract Society, 1928) pp. 251-252

1:16). It was through the preaching of the gospel by the apostles that God besought men to reconcile themselves to their Creator. Paul is not talking about the Watch Tower Society, the 144,000 or the Christ (Jesus plus the 144,000). Maintaining the context is essential to properly interpreting and understanding the Bible.

Reconcile, Reconciled, reconciliation - words of such beauty, signifies the making of friends again. This word implies that friendship was once a reality between God and man; however, something caused rift in that relationship. That *'something,'* was Adam's sin (Isaiah 59:1-2) - his choosing to transgress God's law. Because of God's love for us, He made friendship possible, through the death of Jesus Christ. God's grace provided a way for mankind to be reconciled to his Creator. Reconciliation not only required the death of Jesus, as well as the shedding of His blood, it also required mediation [see p. 244] - someone who understood both the divine as well as the human side of the issues that separated God from man. Consider the following Scriptures.

> *"For there is one God, and one mediator between God and men, the man, Christ Jesus"* (2 Timothy 2:5)

> *"Let this mind be in you, which was also in Christ Jesus: who, existing in the form of God counted not the being on an equality with God a thing to be grasped"* (Philippians 2:5-6)

"God, who at sundry times and in divers manners spake in time past unto the fathers by the prophets, hath in these last days spoken unto us by His son, whom He hath appointed heir of all things, by whom also He made the worlds; Who being the brightness of His glory and the very image of His person, and upholding all things by the word of His power" (Hebrews 1:1-3).

Jehovah's Witnesses would however disagree with what the Bible says concerning reconciliation, because their understanding is skewed. They have chosen not to believe in the doctrines of the *'Trinity,' 'the immortal soul,'* an *'eternal hell,'* that Jesus is the eternal God, or that the gospel is to be preached now. Instead they have devised a doctrine that will reconcile man other than the way God's Word teaches. Rather than believing the gospel is God's power to save (Romans 1:16), they teach that the Watch Tower Society is God's power to save, in the same way it is taught the Vatican or Salt Lake City is God's power to save.

With regard to what the Bible actually teaches about salvation, the ransom and reconciliation of mankind has from the beginning related to deliverance from sin, not from the Battle of Armageddon. Because of this fact, reconciliation to God is necessary so that man is able once again to be at peace with his Creator. Before He created the universe or mankind, God arranged a plan that would deliver us from our sins and turn us from enemies to friends. This was made possible by the death of Christ upon the cross.

"According as He hath chosen us in Him before the foundation of the world, that we should be holy and without blemish" (Ephesians 1:4).

Before the foundation of the world, God knew Adam would sin, thereby severing our fellowship with Him. God knew before He created the universe that the perfect ransom would have to be given so that friendship with man could once again become a reality. He prepared a plan that would redeem mankind, which was first revealed in Genesis 3:15, before removing Adam from the garden and the tree of life.

"And I will put enmity between thee and the woman, and between thy seed and her seed; it shall bruise thy head, and thou shalt bruise his heel" (Genesis 3:15).

Here God spoke to Eve and the serpent, disclosing that Eve's seed (Christ), would bruise the head of the devil, in other words, Christ would destroy the devil's power over spiritual death. Up until the cross it appeared the devil had won, but the cross confirmed that God had always been in control. It was not the '*Perfect Human Life*' of Jesus that God sought, it was the blood sacrifice that would remit the sins of the world, once and for all time, appeasing God's wrath, and offering reconciliation to mankind.

"For thou wast slain, and hast redeemed us to God by

Thy blood" (Revelation 5:8-9)

"For this is My blood of the New Testament which is shed for many for the remission of sins" (Matthew 26:28)

The Old Covenant sacrifices given by the Israelites, were a pattern of the true sacrifice to be offered under the New Covenant.

"But Christ being come an high priest of good things to come, by a greater and more perfect tabernacle, not made with hands, that is to say, not of this building; neither by the blood of goats and calves, but by His own blood He entered in once into the holy place, having obtained eternal redemption of us. For if the blood of bulls and of goats, and the ashes of an heifer sprinkling the unclean, sanctifies to the purifying of the flesh; how much more shall the blood of Christ, who through the eternal Spirit offered Himself without spot to God, purge your conscience from dead works to serve the living God? And for this cause He is the mediator of the New Covenant, that by means of death, for the redemption of the transgressions that were under the first covenant, they which are called might receive the promise of eternal inheritance. For where a covenant is, there must also of necessity be the death of the testator. For a covenant is of force after men are dead: otherwise

169

it is of no strength at all while the testator liveth. Whereupon even the first covenant was dedicated with blood. For when Moses had spoken every precept to all the people according to the law, he took the blood of calves and of goats, with water, and scarlet wool, and hyssop, and sprinkled the book, and all the people, saying, this is the blood of the covenant which God hath enjoined unto you. Moreover he sprinkled with blood both the tabernacle, and all the vessels of the ministry. And almost all things are by the law purged with blood; and without the shedding of blood is no remission." (Hebrews 9:11-22)

Nowhere in the entire Bible, does God discuss man's requirement to obtain a '*Perfect Human Life.*' Nowhere is it taught that sins are not remitted when blood is shed and repentance forthcoming. Because sin was brought into this world by Adam's transgression, God's holiness could no longer allow fellowship with humanity (Habakkuk 1:13).

"Behold, the Lord's hand is not shortened, that it cannot save; neither His ear heavy, that it cannot hear: but your iniquities have separated between you and your God, and your sins have hid His face from you, that He will not hear" (Isaiah 59:1-2)

The words '*reconcile,*' '*reconciled*' and '*reconciliation,*' mean to '*make friends again.*' In Thayer's Greek-English Lexicon, the verb form *'katallosso'* and 2 Corinthians 5:20 are discussed, *"..do not oppose your return into His favor, but lay hold of that favor now offered you..."* [144] It was God's grace that effected reconciliation to all, through the death of the God/Man Jesus Christ. From that moment forward, God's part of the plan was complete, as Jesus declared upon the cross (*"it is finished"* - John 19:30), and man's part became a reality. Before one is justified, they remain enemies of God; but God has provided the means of reconciliation through the death of His Son, Jesus Christ. Paul points out that our being reconciled is *'to God'* (Romans 5:10). Reconciliation rescues us from God's wrath, as well as provides salvation in this life.

This is why the mediatorship of Jesus is so important in God's plan. Jesus is OUR mediator, and the only mediator (1 Timothy 2:5). As God, and our mediator, Jesus has the authority to establish the terms of reconciliation, according to God, *"This is My beloved Son, in whom I am well pleased, hear ye Him"* (Matthew 17:5; 28:18). The conditions of reconciliation and gaining the benefits of Christ's ransom are laid out in the gospel. Unlike what most have been taught today that a person can be reconciled to God by Faith Alone, there is no such idea taught in the Scriptures.

The doctrine of the Watch Tower, teaches salvation is 'potential' and is not now a reality, yet the Bible teaches otherwise. The Word of God clearly teaches that salvation is

---

[144] Joseph Henry Thayer, **A Greek-English Lexicon of the New Testament** (Baker Book House, 1977), p. 333; Strong's #2644

granted to anyone who accepts and obeys God's pre-requisites to obtaining the benefits of Christ's death. Salvation does not come through a dead faith, but through an active obedient faith such as that of Abraham, Noah, Moses and others (Hebrews 11; James 2:17-26). The Bible teaches that salvation is by grace, through the death of Jesus, God's Son (Romans 5:1-10), not through the Watch Tower Society.

God provided us with the opportunity to be reconciled back to Him, and that only happens through obedience to His will, being added to the true kingdom of God, after we have heard the gospel (Romans 10:17), believed the gospel (Hebrews 11:1), Repented (Luke 13:3), Confessed Christ (Romans 10:9-10) and have been immersed in water in order to have our sins remitted, covered by the blood of the Lamb (Acts 22:16; 2:47). The choice is ours; will we believe what men say, or only what the Bible says?

Reconciliation is not about regaining a *'Perfect Human Life'* so we can live on a fictitious paradise earth forever. Reconciliation means that we have taken the correct steps to ask God for His friendship through our mediator Jesus Christ. In order for Jesus to be our mediator, He must understand both sides of the issue, which means He must be both God and man. As God, Jesus knows the divine side of the issues, - as man He recognizes the human side as well. Therefore, He is able to be fair, by representing both sides of the case.

It is the duty of everyone to know what the Bible teaches

(Romans 1:20). To study it, and know what it really teaches about the ransom and salvation of men. We shouldn't allow anyone like the Jehovah's Witnesses, to convince us the earth will last forever or that Jesus died to give us a '*Perfect Human Life*.' Nor should we allow anyone to convince us that we will get a second chance in the mythical 1,000 year kingdom on earth to redeem ourselves. Jesus died to redeem mankind from his sins; no one is able to redeem themselves in the manner the Jehovah's Witnesses teach.

The Bible doctrine of the ransom and reconciliation is far different than that believed by the Witnesses. Everyone has the opportunity to lay hold of the benefits of Christ's death. The choice is up to the individual, to accept what the Bible really teaches, or to reject it and believe what men teach. Regrettably far too many have and will continue to believe error over the truth.

Summary

Understanding the various terms used by the Witnesses is difficult at best, because their material is meant to be cryptic to the outsider. Some of their doctrines are not meant to be understood until a prospective convert has put his complete trust in the Watch Tower Society.

Their doctrines of the ransom and reconciliation are quite different than what the Bible actually teaches. The Witnesses believe Christ's ransom was given first to the 144,000, then potentially to everyone else after the 1,000 year Day of Judgment. Jesus' ransom only removed the inherited sin of Adam from the 144,000's account. In eternity, 'the Christ' (Jesus + 144,000) will reconcile all men to God, for Jehovah has given them the ministry of reconciliation.

Questions to Consider

1. Is it true that Adam was given a 'Perfect Human Life' that was lost when he sinned?

2. Is it true, that Jesus only became a perfect man upon His baptism?

3. Is it true that Jesus' ransom only remitted Adam's sin inherited by us? If not, then what did His ransom do for us?

4. Is it true that men have inherited Adam's sin? If so, then how are we responsible for eating the fruit of the tree of the knowledge of good and evil, when such a tree does not exist?

5. Explain reconciliation. What is its purpose, and who is required to request it?

6. Does salvation occur through a dead, do nothing faith, or through an active obedient faith? Explain.

APPENDIX

God's Organization

Jehovah's Witnesses do not believe in religion, because they assert that true Christianity is not a religion. [145] It is their misunderstanding of the Scriptures that causes them to believe God set up a *'Theocracy.'* [146] According to the Watch Tower, God's organization is a heavenly one that is expressed on earth through the Watch Tower Society. The leaders of the Society are referred to as the *'Governing Body of Jehovah's Witnesses,'* which consists of the anointed class (members of the 144,000). [147] This body has varied in size with as many as eighteen in the 70's but has since dropped to only eight members who no longer are associated with the 1914 generation. [148]

Another term used to describe the *'Governing Body'* is the *'Faithful and Discreet Slave'* [see p. 235]. As Jehovah's

---

[145] J.F. Rutherford, **Government** (Watch Tower Bible & Tract Society, 1928) pp. 138, 139

[146] **Watch Tower Magazine** (Watch Tower Bible & Tract Society, September 1, 2005) p. 21

[147] Ibid, March 15, 2002, pp. 13, 14

[148] This was a hard and fast rule in the beginning, but with the aging and deaths of the anointed class and no sight of Armageddon, the Watchtower has been forced to change its doctrine and replace board members with average Witnesses.

anointed class, they exercise their authority in all matters of doctrine, guidance and regulation. [149] [150] In the beginning Charles T. Russell was THE 'Faithful and Discreet Slave,' considered the anti-type of Daniel. However, in 1927, the Watch Tower announced the 'Faithful Slave' was a body of anointed Christians, not an individual. [151] Recently at their annual meeting of the Society, it was announced that the Governing Body had received 'new light' concerning the matter of the Governing Body. This 'new light' revealed to them that Jehovah no longer required the body to consist only of anointed Christians (members of the 144,000).' [152] This new revelation is important, since the 1914 generation is no longer among us, the Watch Tower was forced to change its doctrine or admit it was a false prophet.

According to the Jehovah's Witnesses, 'God's Organization' is called His 'universal organization' and 'capital organization' of which Jesus is the head and Adam and Eve were a part of before their fall. [153] This organization they say, is also referred to in the Scriptures as 'The Kingdom.' When Jehovah's Witness publishers and pioneers are 'preaching' door to door, they are speaking about their theocratic organization known as the Watch Tower Society/kingdom/church/bride of Christ.

---

[149] **Watch Tower Magazine** (Watch Tower Bible & Tract Society, June 15, 1964) p. 365

[150] Ibid, August 1, 2001, p. 14

[151] **Jehovah's Witnesses – Proclaimers of God's Kingdom** (Watch Tower Bible & Tract Society, 1993) p. 626

[152] **Watch Tower Magazine** (Watch Tower Bible & Tract Society, July 15, 2013) pp. 20-25

[153] J.F. Rutherford, **Riches** (Watch Tower Bible & Tract Society, 1936) p. 13

Because God informs the Witnesses of His will through this anointed group/body. It is also from this anointed group/body that blessings will come to the rest of the world. The Watch Tower is said to be inspired by Jehovah through His angels to make sure the Witnesses, or great multitude, are taught what they need in '*due time.*' [154]

It is alleged that the great multitude of Witnesses flee to the mountains (Jehovah and Christ) finding refuge in God's organization before the '*winter*' which they call Armageddon (Matthew 24:16, 20). [155] This organization is definitely a hierarchy of Catholic proportions. The Governing Body directs six committees (helpers), and appoints all zone, district and circuit overseers. There are 98 branch (Bethels) offices worldwide, which are divided into thirty global zones, with each zone under the oversight of a '*zone overseer.*' Branch (Bethel) offices are operated by volunteer Witnesses, who take a vow of poverty and support themselves.

This snippet of information should be enough to give the average person a sense of their organization, and should anyone try to tie them down to what it is believed they teach, they will almost always reply that a particular doctrine is '*old light*' [see p. 247], and they no longer believe it. However, keep in mind this is not always the case. While they may have received '*new light*' [see p. 245 & 185], on a particular doctrine, just like the one concerning the governing body no

---

[154] Ibid, p. 316
[155] Ibid, pp. 324, 325

longer requiring anointed members (144,000); it doesn't mean they no longer believe the doctrine, but that they have just contrived a different slant on the doctrine than before.

Now that they no longer believe the *'Governing Body,'* must be composed only of the anointed class (144,000), they still believe that body receives orders directly from God, and that the teachings of the Watch Tower must not be questioned.

Jehovah

Is there anything in a name? According to the Jehovah's Witnesses everything they believe and teach is wrapped up in one name, that being the name Jehovah. It is true, out of all the names and designations we find in the Old Testament that describe God's, and His relationship with mankind, the name Jehovah is used more than any other, approximately 6823 times. It is stated by the Watch Tower Society:

> "To distinguish himself from the many false gods, the true God has given himself a personal name. This sets him apart from all others. "Is not 'God' his name?" some may ask. No, for "God" is merely a title, just as "President," "King" and "Judge" are titles. God's personal name is made known to us through his Word, the Bible, and that name is JEHOVAH." [156]

Jehovah's Witnesses, Pentecostals, Branhamites use this argument that God is a title, not a name. The word 'name' has many connotations, such as:

> A title/proper name; a reputation – in name only; a designation of authority – in the name of the law; an

---

[156] **The Truth that Leads to Eternal Life** (Watch Tower Bible &Tract Society, 1968) p. 17

*appointment – named President of the University; to
classify, characterize, denote, cite, et al.* [157]

It is dishonest to insist that names and titles are two entirely
different things, when the fact is that they are synonymous.
The name/title Jehovah is one of many that describe the
multi-faceted character of God as well as how God deals with
man. When God renewed His promise to Abraham,
concerning the Israelites, Moses was told:

> *"I appeared unto Abraham, unto Isaac, and unto
> Jacob, by the name (designation/title), God
> Almighty,*[158] *but by the name (designation/title)
> JEHOVAH was I not known to them."* (Exodus 6:3)

The Watch Tower forgot, or refused to acknowledge that the
first five books of the Old Testament were written by Moses,
some 430 years after Abraham. Moses was commanded by
God to record by inspiration the things that happened from
the beginning to his day. Moses knew God as *'Jehovah,'* but
Abraham, Isaac and Jacob did not, even though Moses records
the name. This is significant, because the Watch Tower Society
insists that 'Jehovah's Witnesses' have existed since the days
of Abel, claiming he was the first Jehovah's Witness. Yet the

---

[157] **Webster's Dictionary and Thesaurus of the English Language** (Lexicon
Publications, Inc., 1993)

[158] The Hebrew word "El-Shaddai" (Genesis 17:1-2; 13:16; 12:2; 15:5). Derived from the
Hebrew word 'El' which is translated 'God' over 200 times and denotes His wonders
and strength (Ps. 68:35). Shaddai is found some 48 times and is sometimes translated
'breast' which signifies one who nourishes, or supplies (Isaiah 66:10-13).

Patriarchs did not know God by that name for God Almighty (El-Shaddai) had not revealed it to them.

The Hebrew word 'YHWH' has been transliterated in our English versions as '*Jehovah*,' most particularly in the 1901 American Standard Version. The King James Version has translated it 'LORD' in all upper case letters, while the name "*Lord*" is the name '*Adonai*.' The Witnesses misperception continues with the name '*Jehovah*,' concerning Judge Rutherford's view of this name:

> "*There is but one First Cause: "He who is from everlasting to everlasting and "whose name alone is Jehovah" (Psalm 90:3; 83:18). ... The name God appears in the Bible in connection with the beginning of creation (Genesis 1:1). That name especially refers to him as the Creator of heaven and earth and the Giver of breath to all creation.*" [159]

He continues:

> "*By and through his Word, the Bible or Holy Scriptures, God reveals himself to his creatures and discloses thereby his purposes concerning his creatures. The meanings of his names or titles are very significant. His name 'The God' means The Mighty One, the Creator of all things. His name 'Jehovah' means his purpose toward his creatures.*

---

[159] J.F. Rutherford, **Reconciliation** (Watch Tower Bible & Tract Society, 1928) p. 103

His name 'The Almighty God' signifies that his power is without limitation. His name 'The Most High' means that he is the Supreme One and there is none before him. His name 'Father' means that he is the Life-giver. [160]

Now let's get this straight, there are names and there are titles, yet in one breath they claim Jehovah has only one name, and in another breath contend He has more than one. Rutherford says, *"His name 'The God' means The Might One, the Creator of all things."* While in a sense it is true, the English phrase, *'The God,'* finds one of two Hebrew words *'El,'* or *'Elohim.'* The name *'El'* refers to God's might and power, while Elohim is a plural name referring to the Godhead and His covenanting and creative power and authority. Almighty God or God Almighty is a compound name from the Hebrew word *'El-Shaddai.'* *'El'* referring to God's power and might, and *'Shaddai'* denoting God as the all-sufficient blessing and nourishing one. At times the doctrine of the Witnesses is very confusing, since they appear to want to have it both ways, like using the names *'God'* [see p. 237], and *'Jehovah'* [see p. 241], as synonymous designations for the same person, yet claiming Jehovah only has one name.

"How important is God's name? Consider the model prayer that Jesus Christ gave. It begins this way: "Our Father in the heavens, let your name be sanctified." (Matthew 6:9) Later, Jesus prayed to

---

[160] J.F. Rutherford, **Riches** (Watch Tower Bible & Tract Society, 1936) pp. 140, 141

God: "Father, glorify your name." In response, God spoke from heaven, saying: "I both glorified it and will glorify it again." (John 12:28) Clearly, God's name is of the utmost importance. Why, then, have some translators left this name out of their translations of the Bible and replaced it with titles? [161]

Bear in mind that they said, "*Is not 'God' his name?" some may ask. No, for "**God" is merely a title**."?* Then later they said, "*The name God appears in the Bible in connection with the beginning of creation (Genesis 1:1). **That name** especially refers to him as the Creator of heaven and earth and the Giver of breath to all creation*" [Emphasis mine]. If the name '*Jehovah*' is of utmost importance, then why did they choose to use that name only fourteen times in the entire article, while using the name '*God*' twenty-one times? Either the name 'Jehovah' is of utmost importance and is the only name that should be used or it is not.

Yes, the name Jehovah is significant, but it is not the only name or designation. The name '*Jehovah*' refers to God's eternal self-existent and unchangeable nature; as well as to His righteousness, holiness and salvation (Jeremiah 16:21; Psalm 83:18; et al). The Patriarchs only knew God by the names Elohim, El-Shaddai, and Adonai, all of which express the concept of the three fold Godhead, which the Watch Tower

---

[161] **What Does the Bible Really Teach?** (Watch Tower Bible & Tract Society, 2005) p. 195

Society denies.

Another significant issue is that the name '*Jehovah*' is a transliteration of the Hebrew word 'YHWH' which is only found in the Old Testament. Since it is not a Greek word, it is never found in the Greek New Testament, yet the Witnesses have chosen to place a Hebrew word in their New World Translation in place of the Greek word "*Kurios*" (Lord) (Matthew 4:10; Acts 18:25; Romans 11:3; 14:4-6, 8, 11; 1 Thessalonians 5:2; 2 Timothy 4:14; et al). We should never be so overtaken by a dogma that we allow ourselves to become dishonest with the Word of God, just to prove our view.

New Light

Gleaned from Proverbs 4:18, *"But the path of the righteous is like the light of dawn, that shines brighter and brighter until the full day,"* the Witnesses believe this verse refers to their receipt of *'new light'* (Revelation) from God. However, as is usually the case with the Watch Tower's mode of interpretation, they have failed to maintain the context. This verse is not speaking about revelation from God, but the righteous individual's ability to increase his understanding of God's will to live a holy life. God said He is not the author of confusion (1 Corinthians 14:33), and therefore, will not allow His revelation to contradiction itself (Old light vs. New Light), which Watch Tower doctrine often does.

The Witnesses make the claim that they are the only religious group that has the truth, which has been directly revealed to the *'Faithful and Discreet Slave'* (Governing Body of the Watch Tower Society) by Jehovah. God has given the Watch Tower the responsibility of teaching the truth to the Great Crowd class of Witnesses. It is for this reason that all congregations of Jehovah's Witnesses study material that is only produced by the Watch Tower Society. All Witnesses are required to accept without question, all material presented to them for study, because it is the truth, and the only truth. One interesting note concerning Watch Tower material being accepted as the truth without question, is that when their material warns of a particular date for the Battle of Armageddon, and that prophecy never comes to pass, then it is the fault of the average Witness for accepting that date without question.

So staunch are their claims that Proverbs 4:18 refers to new revelation that they continually defend it.

> *"IT IS proof of divine wisdom that, in keeping with Proverbs 4:18, the revealing of spiritual truths has taken place gradually by means of flashes of light. In the preceding article, we saw how this text was fulfilled in apostolic times. If the large body of Scriptural truth had been revealed all at once, it would have been both blinding and confusing – much like the effect of coming out of a dark cave into brilliant sunlight. Moreover, gradually revealed truth strengthens the faith of Christians in a continuous way. It makes ever brighter their hope and ever clearer the pathway they are to tread."* [162]

> *"Regarding progressive spiritual enlightenment, Proverbs 4:18 has proved true. It says, "The path of the righteous ones is like the bright light that is*

---

[162] **Watch Tower Magazine** (Watch Tower Bible & Tract Society, May 15. 1995) p. 15

getting lighter and lighter until the day is firmly established." How thankful we are for the progressive spiritual enlightenment we have experienced!" [163]

"The path of the righteous ones is like the bright light that is getting lighter and lighter until the day is firmly established," states Proverbs 4:18. Yes, Jesus' leadership is progressive, not stagnant. Another way to cooperate with Christ's "brothers" is to have a positive attitude toward any refinements in our understanding of Scriptural truths as published by "the faithful and discreet slave." [164]

If it is true, as the Witnesses contend, that Proverbs 4:18 is speaking about doctrine becoming brighter, then that would imply that it was incomplete, not incorrect. Their founder, Charles Russell, said *'new light' never extinguishes older 'light' but adds to it."* [165] However, this has not been the case since Russell's death. Where once it was taught that the Pyramids were prophetic of the year 1914, *'new light'* removed all reference to the Pyramids. Russell taught that all Witnesses would go to heaven, but *'new light'* closed the door to all but the 144,000. In 2012, *'new light'* did not add to older light, but reverted back to allowing all Witnesses to receive a heavenly home. Now,

---

[163] **Watch Tower Magazine** (Watch Tower Bible & Tract Society, January 15. 2001) p. 18

[164] **Watch Tower Magazine** (Watch Tower Bible & Tract Society, May 15. 2011) p. 27

[165] Charles Russell, **Zion's Watch Tower**, February 1881, pp, 3, 188

they are waiting to understand who the Great Crowd refers to.

Shortly before His death, Jesus informed His disciples that they would receive another Comforter. He was to guide the apostles into ALL TRUTH (John 16:13); that truth has been left to us through the gospel (Jude 3, 2 Timothy 3:16-17; 2 Peter 1:3). Anyone claiming to receive new revelation from God either refuses to accept God's word, or is ignorant of what it teaches.

Salvation

Although the Watch Tower continually lambasts the Roman Catholic Church for its style of religion, the Jehovah's Witnesses also teach and practice a '*works*' type of salvation. That's not to say that works are not important in God's scheme of things. Rather than swing to either extreme, that there are no works, or it's all works, we must maintain a balanced view of God's will. Scripture expresses the fact that there are works of '*The Law*' (Romans 3:20), '*Darkness*' (Romans 13:12), and '*the Flesh*' (Galatians 5:19). God says there are '*First*' works (Revelation 2:5) and there are '*Last*' works (Revelation 2:19). There are '*good*' works (Titus 3:8, 14), '*unfruitful*' works (Ephesians 5:11), '*evil*' works (Colossians 1:21), and '*dead*' works (James 2:17; Hebrews 9:14). But the works '*of God*' are those which every person desiring to please their Creator should concern themselves with (John 6:28-29).

It must be recognized that there are works no Christian should find himself taking part in as they profit nothing. However, there are works that are necessary to prove to God we are worthy of His justification. Only the works of God will provide true salvation of the soul as John indicates that the first work (action) is faith itself (John 6:28-29). An active obedient faith motivates us to do as God commands by repenting of sin

(Luke 13:3; Acts 17:30), confessing Jesus as Lord (Romans 10:9-10), and submitting to water immersion (Romans 6:4-6) in order to contact the saving blood of the Lamb. These are the *'works'* of God because He has so commanded that such steps be taken by every believing man and woman. The types of works not accepted by God are the works of the Law of Moses (Romans 3:20), and works of man's invention (Ephesians 2:8-9); which is what we find in the Catholic Church and the Jehovah's Witnesses - a man invented work's salvation that is not found in the Word of God.

Anyone who has ever spoken to the Witnesses that knock on their door notices that they always focus on world events and the terrible incidents occurring at the time. Even the material they hand out teaches the same thing. Why is that? It is because of their misunderstanding of Jesus' prophecy in Matthew chapter Twenty-Four; *"For nation shall rise up against nation, and kingdom against kingdom; and there shall be famines, and pestilences, and earthquakes, in divers places. All these are the beginning of sorrows"* (Vs. 7-8). According to the Watch Tower Society, nation rose up against nation in the year 1914 when World War I began. [166]

They are always looking for the end of the world, the Battle of Armageddon; that will usher in their version of salvation. Most believe the millennial view of the end of the world. This approach helps the Witnesses bond with others who are also

---

[166] J.F. Rutherford, **Salvation** (Watch Tower Bible & Tract Society, 1939) pp. 12, 13

looking for signs. The Watch Tower Society believes the ransom and reconciliation both lead back to having a 'Perfect Human Life' on paradise earth. The ransom removes inherited sin for the 144,000 which prevents them from obtaining the *'Perfect Human Life.'* Salvation to the Jehovah's Witnesses represents something completely different than what the average person understands the word to mean. They define salvation as; *"Deliverance from impending disaster, and finding of refuge in a place of complete safety."* [167] The place of complete safety they refer to is the Watch Tower Society which they call Noah's Ark and the cities of refuge.

Vine's Dictionary of New Testament Words defines the word salvation in this manner: *"Denotes deliverance, preservation, salvation, of material and temporal deliverance from danger and apprehension; national deliverance/salvation; personal, as from the sea, prison, the flood; of the spiritual and eternal deliverance granted immediately by God; of the present experience of God's power to deliver from the bondage of sin."* Since Jehovah's Witnesses are materialists and do not believe in an immortal soul, they have chosen the alternative definition of the word, like Baptists do with the Greek word *'eis'* ('Because of' rather than 'in order to'). Therefore, salvation to the Jehovah's Witness means *"deliverance from the Battle of Armageddon."*

> *"The Battle of Armageddon will be fought by Jesus Christ and His heavenly host, on one side, against the*

---

[167] J.F. Rutherford, **Salvation** (Watch Tower Bible & Tract Society, 1939) p. 10

Devil and all his forces both visible and invisible, on the other side. That battle will be the expression of God's wrath against all wickedness. Upon the earth there are now billions of people, and naturally it is asked, is there salvation for them? Is there to be found a place of refuge, safety and salvation from the impending and terrible wrath of Almighty God?" [168]

Keep in mind that Jehovah's Witnesses are millennialists, which is why the Battle of Armageddon is part of their doctrine. Found in the book of Revelation, John, through symbolic language discusses the pouring out of the first six vials upon the earth (16:1-13). If the theme of the book is kept in mind as well as the fact that John wrote it in figurative language, not literal, then the true meaning of what is said will be properly understood. The word *"Armageddon"* (Har-Magedon in the Hebrew language) is only found this one time in the Bible. John used it in connection with God's overthrow of evil which occurs on the *'Day of God Almighty'* (vs. 14). The Day of God, the Day of the Lord, are used in connection with Christ's return to Judge the world (2 Peter 3:10, 12; 1 Thessalonians 5:2; 1 Corinthians 5:5). Therefore, what John speaks of in figurative language, in Revelation chapter sixteen, is God's wrath being poured out upon the world on Judgment Day.

It is believed by most Bible scholars that Armageddon is a reference to the mountain of Megiddo since the Hebrew word

---

[168] Ibid, p. 26

har was used in the Old Testament for '*hill*' or '*hill country*.' Many places are used as symbols for concepts. Case in point; Zion refers to Jerusalem and the church, Babylon represents apostasy, Egypt and Sodom are symbolic of wickedness and oppression; while the Euphrates symbolizes the point of origin. Therefore, Megiddo or Armageddon represents victory for God's people against all odds; as is found in Old Testament history (Judges 4-5; 7, 2 Kings 9; 23:39). After all, the key word of the book is 'overcome' (2:7, 11, 17, 26; 3:5, 12, 21; 21:7).

Now one interesting note about the fictitious Battle of Armageddon (in the valley of Megiddo), is that all millennialists who insinuate the reality of such a battle always point at signs of its impeding appearance. Yet, John clearly says, *"Behold, I come as a thief. Blessed is he that watches, and keeps his garments..."* (Revelation 16:15). Speaking of His second coming to Judge the world, Jesus says there will be NO SIGNS because He's coming as a thief (1 Corinthians 5:5; 1 Thessalonians 5:2; 2 Peter 3:10; Matthew 24:42-43). Not to mention the fact that when Jesus returns the earth will be burned up, so there will be no valley of Megiddo to hold a battle (2 Peter 3:10-14). Yet the Witnesses contend they alone will be saved from this mythical battle.

> *"Note now God's provision to hide some people from his wrath which will be expressed during Armageddon, and which people so hidden will be*

carried over to safety and to salvation." [169]

"The great deluge of waters that fell upon the earth as soon as eight persons were safely in the ark pictured the Battle of Armageddon, which shall begin its destructive work when all the 'other sheep' (persons of good will) of the Lord are gathered under the protection of the Lord's organization (Jehovah's Witnesses). This is strong proof that only those who are in Christ and those who are of the 'other sheep' of the Lord, together with the "princes," shall survive Armageddon." [170]

While the Jehovah's Witnesses believe in the false doctrines of original or inherited sin, as well as in a millennial kingdom on earth; the Witnesses have developed a different slant on the millennial kingdom that others have not. To them the purpose of the millennial kingdom is for giving everyone (except Adam, Eve and murderers) a second chance to get it right. Only those who are now Jehovah's Witnesses will escape, which is their idea of being *'saved,'* not from sin, but from the Battle of Armageddon.

Salvation through the Society – The Watch Tower Society defines the word *'salvation'* as deliverance from impending disaster, and the finding of refuge in a place of complete

---

[169] Ibid, p. 27
[170] J.F. Rutherford, **Children** (Watch Tower Bible & Tract Society, 1941) p. 295

safety. [171] The *'place of complete safety'* is a reference to the Watch Tower Society. [172] The only ones who will be saved from Armageddon are those individuals who have submitted themselves to Watch Tower doctrine and have become Jehovah's Witnesses. [173] [174] Like the Catholic Church which teaches its members that all understanding of the Scriptures must come from Headquarters, the Watch Tower Society teaches the same. *"Unless we are in touch with this channel of communication God is using, we will not progress along the road of life, no matter how much Bible reading we do."* [175]

Jehovah's Witnesses are o brainwashed on this point that they believe all non-members receive no guidance from God and therefore are, and will remain lost. [176] They claim one of the requirements for salvation from Armageddon is *"Taking in accurate knowledge of God's purposes,"* particularly, a correct understanding of Christ's role as king of the earth. [177] To become a saved Jehovah's Witness one must study Watch Tower material several times per week. [178]

---

[171] Ibid, p. 10

[172] **Watchtower Magazine** (Watch Tower Bible & Tract Society, February 15, 1983) p. 12

[173] **Our Kingdom Ministry** (Watch Tower Bible & Tract Society, 1990) p. 1

[174] **Watchtower Magazine** (Watch Tower Bible & Tract Society, January 15, 1995) p. 28

[175] Ibid, December 1, 1981, p. 27

[176] Ibid, July 1, 1965, p. 391

[177] Ibid, February 15, 1883, p. 15

[178] **Knowledge that Leads to Everlasting Life** (Watch Tower Bible & Tract Society, 1995) p. 92

Salvation from Original Sin – Although Jehovah's Witnesses have accepted the false doctrine of original inherited sin, [179] [180] they have at least rejected the last tenet of Calvinism referred to as '*once-saved-always-saved*' or eternal security. [181] According to Judge Rutherford, "*Adam's offspring are sinners by reason of inherited sin.*" [182] It was Jesus' ransom price that bought or released the faithful believers (the 144,000) from the condemnation inherent in Adam's original sin, thereby returning these chosen ones to the same condition of Adam before sin entered the Garden. [183]

God's eternal purpose was to first ransom the church, which comprises the members of the body of Christ, the saved (the 144,000). [184] All benefits of Jesus' death will not flow to the 'other sheep' or the 'great crowd' until both kingdoms (Heavenly and Earthly) are established after the Battle of Armageddon. Only then will those of the earthly kingdom be blessed by those of the heavenly kingdom (Jesus and the 144,000). [Note: New Light changed this view in 2012, when the Governing Body decided all Witnesses will now receive a heavenly home].

---

[179] J.F. Rutherford, **Reconciliation** (Watch Tower Bible & Tract Society, 1928) p. 45

[180] **What Does the Bible Really Teach?** (Watch Tower Bible & Tract Society, 2010) p. 53

[181] **Watch Tower Magazine** (Watch Tower Bible & Tract Society, October 1, 1999) p. 17

[182] J.F. Rutherford, **Salvation** (Watch Tower Bible & Tract Society, 1939), p. 169

[183] Charles T. Russell, **The Divine Plan of the Ages** (The Dawn Bible Students Association, 1916) p. 150

[184] J.F. Rutherford, **Salvation** (Watch Tower Bible & Tract Society, 1939) p. 200

Of course none of the tenets of Calvinism are taught in the Bible, including original sin, also known as 'Total Hereditary Depravity.' Passages of Scripture are taken out of context to further this satanic doctrine; a doctrine that Jehovah's Witnesses have accepted though they speak against the beliefs of John Calvin. [185] Salvation to the Jehovah's Witness has many aspects, and release from Adamic sin for the 144,000 anointed ones is only a small piece of the puzzle.

Salvation from Armageddon – The Battle of Armageddon as described in Revelation sixteen, verses 12-16 has been falsely understood as a literal one, when the book itself is apocalyptic symbolism. Russell in his famous series *'Studies of the Scriptures,'* developed the idea that Armageddon would remove religion and civil governments from the earth in order for Jehovah to create a millennial kingdom that would exist for the converting of the world. [186] Russell asserted that Armageddon would appear in 1914, which Rutherford then changed to 1925, and the Watch Tower eventually predicting its imminent coming in 1954, [187] as evidenced by their publications which continually ask the question, *"Are we living in the last days?"*

Jehovah's Witnesses teach that *'Babylon the Great'* [see p. 223], will be destroyed by the beast (civil government) prior to

---

[185] **Watch Tower Magazine** (Watch Tower Bible & Tract Society, October 1, 2006) p. 8

[186] Charles T. Russell, **Studies in the Scriptures, Vol. IV, The Battle of Armageddon** (Watchtower Bible & Tract Society, 1916). p. Dxv-D14

[187] **You May Survive Armageddon into God's New World** (Watch Tower Bible & Tract Society, 1955), p. 11

Armageddon, then it will turn to destroy the Witnesses, but God will intervene destroying all forms of human government, binding Satan for 1000 years, and establishing His rule on earth during that time. [188] [189] Jehovah's Witnesses believe their purpose in this life is to *'preach'* the good news of the coming kingdom of God [190] so they may 'save' non-Witnesses from destruction in the Battle of Armageddon. [191]

Salvation through works – The average Jehovah's Witness is not of the anointed class (the 144,000) and therefore must work out their salvation with fear and trembling (Philippians 2:12), as they like to quote. 'Preaching' is one of the important 'works' required by every Witness who desires to be saved from Armageddon. After months of study, and acceptance of Watch Tower doctrine, an unbaptized publisher may ask to become a baptized publisher (Jehovah's Witness). He will go before the local eldership for a four hour Q & A session so they are sure he truly accept their doctrine, as well as making sure he is a serious publisher; who has *'preached'* (knocked doors and set up studies) no less than 20 hours per month.

Documenting their amount of preaching is difficult, since it is not written in their material. Most of what has been learned about their *'works'* was discovered on ex-Jehovah's Witness blogs and websites. There is no intention of taking their beliefs

---

[188] **Mankind's Search for God** (Watch Tower Bible & Tract Society, 1990) pp. 371-376

[189] **Watch Tower Magazine** (Watch Tower Bible & Tract Society, September 15, 2005) p. 19

[190] **What Does the Bible Really Teach?** (Watch Tower Bible & Tract Society, 2010) p. 92

[191] Ibid, pp. 94, 95

out of context, and if such is found, then it is completely by mistake, since their doctrines are ever evolving due to the *'new light'* (Revelations) the Watch Tower Society supposedly receives from Jehovah. [192] [193] [194]

Following are additional quotes from Watch Tower material that reveals more about their doctrine of salvation:

> *"If we stop actively supporting Jehovah's work, then we start following Satan. There is no middle ground." Watchtower* 2011 Jul 15 p.18

> *"But Jehovah's servants already belong to the only organization that will survive the end of this wicked system of things." Watchtower* 2007 Dec 15 p.14

> *"But if we were to draw away from Jehovah's organization, **there would be no place else to go for salvation** and true joy." Watchtower* 1993 Sep 15 p.22 [Emphasis mine]

> ***"Only Christian witnesses of Jehovah** who successfully pass this test will survive and come forth like fire-refined gold for God's use in his precious*

---

[192] **Watch Tower Magazine** (Watch Tower Bible & Tract Society, February 15, 1983) pp. 12, 13

[193] **You can Live Forever in Paradise Earth** (Watch Tower Bible & Tract Society, 1982) p. 133

[194] **Pay Attention to Yourselves and to all the Flock** (Watch Tower Bible & Tract Society, 1991) pp. 35, 51, 61, 98, 99

new order." *Watchtower* 1985 Mar 1 p.14 [Emphasis mine]

*"And while now the witness yet includes the invitation to **come to Jehovah's organization for salvation**, the time no doubt will come when the message takes on a harder tone, like a "great war cry.""* Watchtower 1981 Nov 15 p.21 [Emphasis mine] *"But Jehovah God has also provided his visible organization, his "faithful and discreet slave", made up of spirit-anointed ones, to help Christians in all nations to understand and apply properly the Bible in their lives. Unless we are in touch with this channel of communication that God is using, **we will not progress along the road to life, no matter how much Bible reading we do**." Watchtower* 1981 Nov 15 p.27 [Emphasis mine]

*"They must appreciate that identifying themselves with **Jehovah's organization is essential to their salvation**." Kingdom Ministry* 1990 Nov p.1 [Emphasis mine]

*"**Direct Interest Progressively on Bible Studies:** The primary purpose of a Bible study is to teach the truth of God's Word. It should also build in the student an appreciation for Jehovah's organization and make him aware of **the vital need to become part of it**. ... The weekly Bible study*

should include instruction that will help students appreciate the organization and take advantage of **provisions for their salvation**. *Take a few minutes each week to relate or describe something about the organization and how it functions. You can find helpful talking points in the November 1, 1984, Watchtower. The brochures Jehovah's Witnesses in the Twentieth Century and Jehovah's Witnesses Unitedly Doing God's Will Worldwide discuss major facets of the organization and how they may benefit us. Arranging for Bible students to view the video Jehovah's Witnesses the Organization behind the Name will let them see for themselves what it is accomplishing." Kingdom Ministry* 1993 Apr p.3 [Emphasis mine]

The Archangel Michael

Jehovah's Witnesses believe Jesus was created by God as the first of His angels in heaven, along with his brother Lucifer. They say that Jehovah then allowed Jesus to create the rest of the angels and the universe. Because they falsely assume Jesus is created, they have incorrectly concluded Jesus is an Archangel. Listen to their words.

> *"....The Bible indicates that Michael is another name for Jesus Christ, before and after his life on earth. Let us consider Scriptural reasons for drawing this conclusion. God's word refers to Michael "the archangel." (Jude 9) This term means "chief angel." Notice that Michael is called the archangel. This suggests that there is only one such angel. In fact, the term "archangel" occurs in the Bible only in the singular, never in the plural. Moreover, Jesus is linked with the office of archangel. Regarding the resurrected Lord Jesus Christ, 1 Thessalonians 4:16 states: "The Lord himself will descend from heaven with a commanding call, with an archangel's voice." Thus the voice of Jesus is described as being that of an archangel. This scripture therefore suggests that*

Jesus Himself is the archangel Michael." [195]

They assert without cause, that since Paul says Jesus will be accompanied with *"the voice of an archangel,"* that means He is the archangel (1 Thessalonians 4:16). If that is the basis of their reasoning, then the text also says Jesus will be accompanied with a shout and with the trump of God, so logically speaking, and according to their reasoning, Jesus is also the trump of God – if not, why not? To demonstrate that Jesus is not an angel, or archangel; we turn to the book of Hebrews where the author states clearly that God did not give authority to angels but to the God/Man Jesus Christ who is superior over the angels.

> *"For unto which of the angels said He at any time, Thou art My Son, this day have I begotten Thee? And again, I will be to Him a Father, and He shall be to Me a Son? And again, when He bringeth the first-begotten into the world, he saith, And let all the angles of God worship Him. And of the angels He saith, Who maketh His angels spirits, and His ministers a flame of fire.* **But unto the Son He saith, Thy throne, <u>O God</u>, is for ever and ever:** *a scepter of righteousness is the scepter of Thy kingdom. Thou hast love righteousness, and hated iniquity; therefore God, even Thy God, hath anointed Thee with the oil of gladness above Thy fellows. And Thou, Lord, in the beginning hast laid the foundation*

---

[195] Ibid, pp. 218, 219

of the earth; and the heavens are the works of Thine hands: they shall perish; but Thou remainest; and they all shall wax old as doth a garment; and as a vesture shalt Thou fold them up, and they shall be changed; but Thou art the same, and Thy years shall not fail. But to which of the angels said He at any time, Sit on My right hand, until I make Thine enemies Thy footstool?" (Hebrews 1:5-13) [Emphasis mine)

*"For **NOT UNTO ANGELS** did He subject the world to come, whereof we speak."* (Hebrews 2:5) [Emphasis mine)

Notice that God the Father is speaking to God the Son by referring to Jesus as '*God*' (Greek word '*Theos*'), which is the same word used for God the Father. Jesus is also called '*Lord*' (Greek word '*Kurie*') a term of respect that denotes sovereignty, which only Jehovah God possesses. Jesus is not Michael the Archangel, or any other angel. He is the eternal, self-existent creator of the universe and savior of mankind. He is as much Jehovah God as is God the Father, and God the Holy Spirit. With the mishandling of prophecies and scriptures, Jehovah's Witnesses can only assert without facts, that Michael was Jesus's name in heaven. But the truth will always prevail as it does in the case.

Judge Rutherford however, maintaining the philosophy of his predecessor Charles Russell, stated:

"No creature can exist without form or organism. Every being must have a body suited to that being or creature. "There is a natural body, and there is a spiritual body." (1 Corinthians 15:44) The natural body is flesh and blood and bones. A spirit body has none of these. (Luke 24:39; 1 Corinthians 15:50) Man cannot describe the appearance of a spirit body, because this knowledge has not been given nor revealed to him. "It doth not yet appear" what a spirit being is like. – 1 John 3:2. ..... Seraphim is the name given to other creatures of the spirit realm. They were created by the Logos, acting in the name and under the direction of the great Jehovah God. These creatures are bearers of light reflecting the glory of the great Jehovah. – Isaiah 6:2-4. Archangel is the name given to some of God's spirit creatures, which name signifies "First in rank." (1 Thessalonians 4:16) The title or name archangel was also applied at times to the Logos, when he was serving Jehovah in a certain or specific capacity."[196]

Their doctrine is a mass of confusion. They conclude that the name Archangel is only given to those spirit creatures that are first in rank! Notice he said spirit 'creatures,' (plural). This doctrine of course only furthers their perception that Jesus is not God, but 'a' god, the first of Jehovah God's creation, [197]

---

[196] J.F. Rutherford, **Creation** (Watch Tower Bible & Tract Society, 1927) pp. 14, 15
[197] **Let God be True** (Watch Tower Bible & Tract Society, 1948) p. 32

and one of two sons, the second being Lucifer. [198] In order for Jesus to match their timeline he had to become 'Michael,' so their twist on prophecy would make sense. Pay attention once again to what Judge Rutherford says on this subject:

> *"..corroborated by the prophecy of Daniel wherein it is stated that Michael began his activities against Satan. "Michael" means the Anointed One of God, which is Christ Jesus. The prophet said: "And at that time [to wit, at the end of the world, in 1914, or the 'beginning of sorrows'] shall Michael stand up, the great prince which standeth for the children of thy people; and there shall be a time of trouble, such as never was since there was a nation even to that same time." (Daniel 12:1) ..... The birth of the "man child" symbolically represents The Government and marks the time when Christ's government began its activity against Satan. The first act of that new government was to oust Satan from heaven. "And there was war in heaven: Michael and his angels fought against the dragon; and the dragon fought against his angels, and prevailed not; ......" (Revelation 12:7-10).* [199]

> *"Before 2 B.C. God's only-begotten Son in heaven was called Michael, this name meaning "Who is like God?" When he emptied himself of his heavenly*

---

[198] Ibid, p. 48

[199] J.F. Rutherford, **Government** (Watch Tower Bible & Tract Society, 1928), pp. 179-181

powers and his life was miraculously transferred to the womb of the virgin Jewess Mary and he was born and called Jesus, did he forfeit his heavenly name Michael? No! Before the birth of Jesus there are ten men in the nation of Israel who were listed with the name Michael (Numbers 13:13; 1 Chronicles 5:13-14, 6:40, 7:3; 8:16; 12:20, 27:18; Ezra 8:8; 2 Chronicles 21:2), yet the Son of God was not to be known on earth by that name. ....When he died as the man Jesus Christ and was resurrected and went back to heaven, what was his proper name? Was it still or was it only Jesus Christ? No; it was not just his earthly human name. He resumed his heavenly name Michael. The name Jesus Christ was retained in order to show his identicalness with the human-born Son of God on earth."[200]

First of all, the idea that name '*Michael*' means, "*anointed one of God*," is false, the true meaning of the name is "*Who is like God.*" Now if it is true that Michael was the heavenly name of the Logos before he came to earth, then why does the Watch Tower Society not refer to him by that name in their material? Jesus is the only name they use, which is quite odd, given he had a heavenly name and an earthly name. This is common with the Watch Tower and Witnesses, talking out of both sides of their mouth. Saying Jesus' heavenly name was Michael, but never referring to him that way, and saying Jehovah is God's

---

[200] **Your Will be Done on Earth** (Watch Tower Bible & Tract Society, 1958), pp. 315, 316

only name, yet using the word God more times than the word Jehovah.

Jehovah's Witnesses find themselves in a dilemma, even though their Bible translation causes them to think they have solved any doctrinal problems. They argue Jesus, the Logos, is not God Almighty, but '*a*' god, meaning, '*a*' mighty one. [201] Yet they quote Exodus 20:2; "..*Thou shalt have no other gods before Me.*" And Isaiah 42:8, "*there is no God beside Me.*" This is only a small piece of the confusion that is rampant in Watch Tower doctrine. They try very hard to make us believe that an angel is '*a*' god. Can't be both, either '*Michael*' is an angel or he is '*a*' god, the law of excluded middle can't be broken.

---

[201] J.F. Rutherford, **Riches** (Watch Tower Bible & Tract Society, 1936), p. 12

The Cross

The doctrine of the '*cross*,' is one of several doctrines in which the Watch Tower Society continually receives '*new light*.' At their inception, they readily accepted the fact that Jesus died on a cross. Then in 1931 Judge Rutherford received new revelation that they had been wrong.

> "*Beginning with its issue of October 15, 1931, The Watch Tower no longer bore the cross and crown symbol on its cover. A few years later Jehovah's people first learned that Jesus Christ did not die on a T-shaped cross. On January 31, 1936, Brother Rutherford released to the Brooklyn Bethel family the new book Riches. Scripturally, it said, in part, on page 27: 'Jesus was crucified, not on a cross of wood, such as is exhibited in many images and pictures, and which images are made and exhibited by me: Jesus was crucified by nailing his body to a tree.*" [202]

In 1937, Judge Rutherford published yet another book entitled '*Enemies*,' where he stated that: "*Jesus was not crucified on a*

---

[202] **1975 Yearbook of Jehovah's Witnesses** (Watch Tower Bible & Tract Society) pp. 148, 149

cross." [203] Then just two years later, Judge Rutherford cited Philippians 2:8-11 asserting that Jesus' death was upon the cross, not a torture stake. [204] To further their agreement with the Judge, the Watch Tower described their idea of the crucifixion in this way.

> *"His hands being held, one upon the other, until the spike punctured and tore through the flesh to embed itself in the wood. The red of his blood beginning to stain his hands when another spike was driven through his feet. Then the stake being swung upright until his whole weight hung on these two points."* [205]

Like all of their doctrines, the Watch Tower Society uses only selected narrations that agree with their beliefs. In this case they cite the Plymouth Brethren's W.E. Vine, who defines '*stauros*' (cross), as being an upright pale or stake, as distinguished from the ecclesiastical form of a two beamed cross. [206] The Watch Tower also cites The Expository Dictionary of New Testament Words and The Encyclopedia Britannica to prove their case that it was a 'torture stake' and not a cross. [207]

---

[203] J.F. Rutherford, **Enemies** (Watch Tower Bible & Tract Society, 1937) p. 187

[204] J.F. Rutherford, **Salvation** (Watch Tower Bible & Tract Society, 1939) p. 40

[205] **Watchtower Magazine** (Watch Tower Bible & Tract Society, April 1, 1965) p. 211

[206] **Vine's Expository Dictionary of New Testament Words**, Greek word 'σταυροσ' (Thomas Nelson, 1996)

[207] **Make Sure of All Things – Hold Fast to What is Fine** (Watch Tower Bible & Tract Society, 1965) pp. 139, 140

Appendix

Historians and Archeologists have shown that several variations of the 'cross' were used through the centuries (trees, stakes, T-shaped and X-shaped). [208] However, Biblical evidence seems to prove that it was the T-shaped cross upon which Jesus was crucified, as Kittel explains the use of the word 'stauros.'

> "Crucifixion took place as follows. The condemned person carried the patibulum (cross-beam) to the place of execution – the stake already erected. Then on the ground he was bound with outstretched arms to the beam by ropes, or else fixed to it by nails. The beam was then raised with the body and fastened to the upright post." [209]

This certainly seems to fit the accounts we are given by Matthew, Mark, Luke and John. As it is written:

> "And as they came out, they found a man of Cyrene, Simon by name: him they compelled to bear His cross (patibulum)." (Matthew 27:32)

> "And they compel one Simon a Cyrenian, who passed by, coming out of the country, the father of Alexander and Rufus, to bear His cross (patibulum)." (Mark 15:21)

---

[208] Michael Green, **Evangelism in the Early Church**, pp. 214, 215
[209] Gerhard Kittel, **Theological Dictionary of the New Testament**, Vol. VII, p. 573

"And as they led Him away, they laid hold upon one Simon, a Cyrenian, coming out of the country, and on him they laid the cross (patibulum), that he might bear it after Jesus." (Luke 23:26)

"Then delivered he (Pilate) him therefore unto them to be crucified. And they took Jesus, and led Him away. And He bearing His cross (patibulum) went forth into a place called the place of the skull, which is called in the Hebrew Golgotha." (John 19:16-17)

While it could be argued that Simon was carrying the upright post that would be used to *'impale'* Jesus and would then be raised up to be sat down into a hole, there is more evidence for the T-shaped cross. As Kittel states, it was the *'cross-beam'* (*patibulum*) that Simon carried to the crucifixion site to which Jesus' hands were nailed and then it was raised up to sit upon the upright post. The Watch Tower however describes their version of crucifixion where His hands were held above His head to be nailed to the stake, then His feet were nailed before the stake was lifted up. Yet, what does the inspired record tell us concerning His hands when Jesus appeared to His disciples?

"The other disciples therefore said unto him (Thomas), We have seen the Lord. But he said unto them, Except I shall see in His hands the print of the **nails**, *and put my finger into the print of the* **nails**, *and thrust my hand into His side, I will not believe."*

(John 20:25) [Emphasis mine]

The Watch Tower says Jesus's hands were held together and '*a*' spike driven through them. Notice that Thomas uses the plural form of the word '*nail*,' and the singular form of the word '*print*' or '*imprint*.' This usage would mean that a single imprint was made in each hand by a nail (spike), meaning there was more than one nail (spike) used. We also find the Watch Tower asserting that Jesus's hands were above His head when impaled, yet the inspired record implies His hands were below head level, meaning they were stretched out on a horizontal plane. The only mention of anything being over His head was the accusation.

> *"And set up **over His head** His accusation written, THIS IS JESUS THE KING OF THE JEWS."* (Matthew 27:37) [Emphasis mine]

Would it not be logical, that if Jesus were crucified in the manner argued by the Jehovah's Witnesses, that the text should read "*over his hands?*" There is enough evidence Biblically and secularly that offers positive proof that Jesus was crucified upon a T-shaped cross and that it is not something Christians later accepted from the pagans.

The Lord's Evening Meal

Every year, Jehovah's Witnesses the world over gather to commemorate the death of Jesus. They say, *"On the night before he surrendered his life, Jesus instructed his faithful followers to remember, or commemorate, his sacrifice. Using the unleavened bread and the red wine before them, he instituted what has been called the Last Supper or the Lord's Evening Meal and commanded "Keep doing this in remembrance of me"* (Luke 22:19). [210]

Each year they invite non-Witnesses to attend this event on the Thursday before Easter and after sunset. Having personally attended one of these events, I found it very interesting to witness what occurred. After everyone gathers, sometimes at a local hotel conference room or ballroom, as was the case where I attended, they sing hymns with recorded instrumental music. Then a speaker tells about the significance of the gathering for evening meal. Several men then stand to offer prayer for the unleavened bread, which is then passed around the room, after which prayer is offered for the 'red wine' (alcohol) and that too, is passed around the room. What I found as being odd, was that not one person

---

[210] **Watch Tower Magazine** (Watch Tower Bible & Tract Society, March 1, 2008) back cover

partook of either. Why you might ask? Because the memorial meal is only to be taken by the anointed class, the church, the 144,000.

Strangely, some Witnesses consider this more of a '*rejection*' ceremony, since every Witness attending the event rejects taking the emblems. What is the point for requiring the '*great crowd*' class to attend such an event that they are unable to partake, but must reject? Where do they get the idea that this is to be observed annually after sunset? They argue that since Passover was an annual event when the supper was instituted, then the '*evening meal*' should also be taken annually. Calling it the '*evening meal*' comes from their mistranslating 1 Corinthians 11:25 "*after supper*" to "*evening meal.*" [211] It is clear from the Scriptures that the Lord's Supper was to be observed more than once a year, that the emblems were to be taken by every believer, and that the 'cup' (Fruit of the vine) was not alcoholic.

Writing to the Christians in Corinth, Paul instructed them "*Do this, **as often** as you drink it, in remembrance of Me*" (1 Corinthians 11:25) [emphasis mine]. Then again he wrote, "*For **as often** as you eat this bread, and drink this cup, you proclaim the Lord's death until He comes*" (vs. 26) [emphasis mine]. Paul's use of the Greek words 'hosakis ean' denotes indefinite and multiple points of time. [212] To understand how

[211] Ibid, February 1, 2011, pp. 21, 22
[212] Johannes P. Louw and Eugene A. Nida, **Greek-English Lexicon of the New Testament Based on Semantic Domains, 2nd Ed.** (United Bible Societies, 1989)

often the Supper was taken in the first century, we find in Acts 20:7 that the Christians in Troas specifically *came together* (Assembled) on the first day of every week (Sunday) for the purpose of observing the Lord's Supper. While the Jews celebrated Passover annually, Christians are commanded to observe the Lord's Supper weekly in order to proclaim His death to the world until His return (1 Corinthians 11:26).

The Year 1914

In October of the year 1914, World War broke out in Europe between reigning family members. Charles T. Russell mishandled the prophecy of Matthew chapter Twenty-Four by applying Jesus' warning to the Jews of the first century, to WWI. According to the Witnesses, this was the year Jesus was set upon His throne, and the Battle of Armageddon would begin to rid the world of Satan's organization (World governments and religion). Bear in mind in the last year or so the Watch Tower has since downgraded the importance of the year 1914.

There are several designations used by the Jehovah's Witnesses for the year 1914, *'The Day of Jehovah,'* [213] *'The Appointed time of the nations,'* [214] *'The seven times,'* [215] *'The establishment of God's kingdom in the heavens,'* [216] *and 'the Gentile Times.'* [217] Their calculations for determining the year 1914 as the end of the *'Gentile Times'* [see p. 235], and the beginning of the kingdom of God, are loosely based upon a false interpretation of Nebuchadnezzar's reign as king of Babylon.

---

[213] Ibid, p. 319
[214] **Your Will be Done on Earth** (Watch Tower Bible & Tract Society, 1958) p. 105
[215] Ibid, p. 126
[216] Ibid, p. 212
[217] Ibid, p. 268

"Nebuchadnezzar is reported to have reigned for forty-three years. So these 'seven times' of insanity in between must have been seven years at the most, in his personal case. In the Holy Bible a "time" is used in places to stand for a literal year (Daniel 7:25; 12:7). ...How long then are these "seven times?" .. In Nebuchadnezzar's case a "time" stood for a lunar year, the average of which was reckoned as 360 days. ...On this basis, then, a lunar year of 360 days would stand for 360 years, (Numbers 14:34; Ezekiel 4:6)... "Seven Times," symbolically speaking, would amount to 2,560 literal years...would end in the early fall of the year 1914 A.D." [218]

Like all date setters, the Watch Tower Society applies faulty math, not to mention, adding to the words of the prophets, which is the problem with all millennial doctrine; always going beyond what God intended. Not one word is mentioned in the text of Daniel 7 & 12 about *'seven times.'* Daniel did say *"time, and time, and half a time"* (3 ½), but not seven. Both Daniel and Jesus (Matthew 24) spoke of the destruction of the literal city of Jerusalem by Rome in 70 A.D.

However the Witnesses assert that Jesus and Daniel are speaking of the destruction of the world in 1914 at the Battle called Armageddon which then begins the 1,000 year reign of *'the Christ'* in heaven. Charles T. Russell emphatically declared that the year 1914 was not the beginning of the end,

---

[218] Ibid, pp. 100, 101

but would be the very end of the world. [219]

After Russell's death in 1916, and the failure of the end of the world to come to pass in 1914, Judge Rutherford changed from an emphatic end, to the year 1914 being the *'beginning'* of the end. [220] [221] October 1914 marked the end of Satan's organization in the Battle of Armageddon, and the establishment of God's organization both heavenly and earthly. When that didn't occur, they began to say it started then, but would be a continual process.

> *"The years from 1914 to 1918 did, indeed, prove to be a "testing season" for the Bible Students. Some of the tests came from within; others came from outside. .... There were also other expectations concerning 1914. Alexander H. Macmillan, who had been baptized in September 1900, later recalled: "A few of us seriously thought we were going to heaven during the first week of October." In fact, recalling the morning that Russell announced the end of the Gentile Times, Macmillan admitted: "We were highly excited and I would not have been surprised if at that moment we had just started up, that becoming the signal to begin ascending heavenward – but of course there was*

---

[219] **Watch Tower Magazine** (Watch Tower Bible & Tract Society, 1894), p. 1677

[220] J.F. Rutherford, **Prophecy** (Watch Tower Bible & Tract Society, 1929) p. 52

[221] **What Does the Bible Really Teach?** (Watch Tower Bible & Tract Society, 2005) p. 218

nothing like that." [222]

The reason the Witnesses claim God changed His mind by not ending the world (religion and civil government) in 1914, was because God decided his witnesses first needed to *'preach'* warnings (serve notice) to the peoples of the earth. [223] What does the Watch Tower Society now declare about the year 1914? At first they began with a <u>firm</u> assertion that 1914 was THE date for the Battle of Armageddon and the end of the world. [224]

Upon their prophetic failure however, they tailored their doctrine to pronounce 1914 as the *'beginning'* of the end and that the *"last generation"* (those Witnesses born before 1914) would see the Battle of Armageddon before they died. [225] The Faithful and Discreet Slave Class (members of the 144,000) in 1995 abandoned that idea and changed the meaning of the word *'generation'* to denote unlimited human lifespans. [226] Fifteen years later they received *'new light'* (revelation) and pronounced that generations overlap one another. [227] Now, in just three short years, the Watch Tower Society admits they have been wrong all along.

---

[222] **Jehovah's Witnesses – Proclaimers of God's Kingdom** (Watch Tower Bible & Tract Society, 1993), pp. 61, 62

[223] J.F. Rutherford, **Government** (Watch Tower Bible & Tract Society, 1928) p. 279

[224] Charles T. Russell, **The Time is at Hand** (Watch Tower Bible & Tract Society, 1889) p. 101

[225] **Watch Tower Magazine** (Watch Tower Bible & Tract Society, May 15, 1984) pp. 6, 7

[226] Ibid, Nov. 1, 1995, pp. 17-20

[227] Ibid, June 15, 2010, p. 5

For a number of years, we thought that the great tribulation began in 1914 with World War I and that "those days were cut short" by Jehovah in 1918 when the war ended so that the remnant would have the opportunity to preach the good news to all nations. (Matt. 24:21, 22) After the completion of that preaching work, Satan's empire would be destroyed.... Upon further examination of Jesus' prophecy, however, we perceived that a part of Jesus' prophecy about the last days has two fulfillments..... It was noted that Jesus became King of God's Kingdom in 1914, but he did not "sit down on his glorious throne" as Judge of "all the nations." (Matt. 25:32; compare Daniel 7:13.)... Matthew 24:17. What have we stated about the arrival mentioned at Matthew 24:46? A consideration of Jesus' prophecy in its entirety leads us to what conclusion about Jesus' coming? .... Matthew 24 also applies to his future coming, during the great tribulation. [228]

While they make the claim to be God's prophet, they are not doing a very good job of revealing God's will to its members. Matthew chapter Twenty-Four is divided into the answering of three questions asked of Jesus by His disciples. #1 – *"When will the destruction of the temple occur?"* (vs. 3) #2&3 – "What will be the sign of Jesus' return, and the end of the world?" (vs. 3). Jesus answers these questions in succession beginning with the first answer found in verses four through

---

[228] **Watch Tower Magazine** (Watch Tower Bible & Tract Society, 2013) pp. 3, 4, 6, 8

thirty-five. There He is speaking of His judgment upon the Jews for their unbelief with the destruction of Jerusalem by the Romans in AD70. In verse thirty-four Jesus states, *"Verily I say unto you (those listening to Him), This generation (first century) shall not pass, UNTIL all these things be fulfilled."*

Bible interpretation must not be taken lightly, each time the word *'you'* is found in a text, does not mean it is speaking directly to those reading it. Context must always be considered, and in this case the context clearly reveals who Jesus was speaking to when He said, *"This generation."* It was not Russell's generation in the late 19th century, any more than it is our generation of the 21st century. Jesus meant the generation He was speaking to, and nothing more. World War I was never intended to be part of the context.

In verses 36-51 of Matthew twenty-four, on into chapter Twenty-Five, Jesus answers the last two questions from His disciples about His return and the end of the world. Concerning Jesus being given the throne of David in 1914 and then not sitting upon it until later? This interpretation ignores many passages of Scripture that teach the opposite. God said Jesus' throne would be forever (Hebrews 1:8), **until** His enemies became His footstool (Hebrews 1:13), at which time He would return the kingdom to God (1 Corinthians 15: 24-25). What king does not have a throne (1 Timothy 1:17; 6:15)? Jesus sat upon His throne at the right hand of God after ascending into heaven in 30AD, never having to wait 1884 years to *'begin'* sitting upon it (Acts 2:33; Hebrews 1:3; 8:1). It does appear however that the Witnesses are finished giving specific dates to any end time events. Then again, the Watch Tower blames its readers for believing the dates they have set. Despite Scriptural proof to the contrary, the Witnesses still hold 1914 as the date that Jesus was given his throne in heaven.

Questions for Jehovah's Witnesses To Consider

1. It is the case that Jehovah's Witnesses believe death is the cessation of existence. They say hell, the grave, and destruction, are a condition of death which is annihilation. If this is true, why did God prohibit the practice of necromancy (seeking after the dead)?

2. It is the case that Jehovah's Witnesses believe death is the cessation of existence as did the Sadducees. Therefore, Jehovah's Witnesses are confronted by the same dilemma as the Sadducees when Jesus told them: *"Ye do err, not knowing the Scriptures, or the power of God. .... Have ye not read that which was spoken unto you by God, saying, I am the God of Abraham, and the God of Isaac, and the God of Jacob? God is not the God of the dead, but of the living?"*

3. It is the case that Jehovah's Witnesses believe death is the cessation of existence, annihilation. Therefore according to their doctrine Jesus did not rise from the grave in the body that was placed in the tomb. If this is true, then why was such emphasis placed on the empty tomb? Why did Paul use this event to prove the

resurrection of the saints (1 Corinthians 15:1-20)? Why did the Jews pay the soldiers to say Jesus' body was stolen (Matthew 28:12-13).

4. It is the case that Jehovah's Witnesses believe Jehovah God the Father is the only person in the Godhead. That He created two sons, the Logos and Lucifer. If it is true that Jesus and the devil are equal spirit beings, then why were the demons afraid of Jesus' power? (Mark 3:22-30; 5:1-14).

5. It is the case that Jehovah's Witnesses do not believe in the concept of the 'trinity,' because the word is not found in the Bible. Where is the name "Jehovah's Witness" found in the Bible?

6. It is the case that Jehovah's Witnesses do not believe Jesus is God. Then why did the Jews try to stone Him for blasphemy when Jesus equated Himself with God? (Matthew 9:3; Mark 2:7; John 10:33).

7. It is the case that Jehovah's Witnesses do not believe Jesus is God. Then why did Thomas, upon examining the evidence before him, declare Jesus as, "My Lord and my God?" (John 20:28)

8. It is the case that Jehovah's Witnesses believe only the 144,000 will sit on thrones in heaven along-side Jesus. They call them the "little flock." But the 'great crowd'

will inherit a 'Perfect Human Life' on paradise earth forever. The Great Crowd will never see Jesus or heaven. If this is true, then why did John see both the 144,000 AND the 'great crowd' before the throne? (Revelation 14:1-3; 19:1-6).

9. It is the case that all Witnesses must obey the Watch Tower Society by keeping its laws. Are they keeping God's Laws? If not, why not? Is this not disobedience to the Watch Tower, and therefore a sin?

10. If the term "Son of God" means that Jesus is not God, then does the term "Son of man" mean Jesus was not a man? If not, why not?

11. It is the case that Witnesses believe that salvation is not granted in this life. It is their HOPE, that God will grant them salvation after the millennial reign. Yet they believe that salvation can be lost. If this is the case, then how, is it possible to lose salvation, when you don't have it in the first place?

Glossary of Terms

Antichrist – According to the Watch Tower Society all people, organizations, or groups that falsely claim to represent Christ or oppose Christ and his disciples (JW's) can properly be called antichrists. [229]

Anointed – Witnesses believe this word is used to show the pouring out of 'holy spirit' on those persons chosen for the heavenly hope (the 144,000). [230] It also refers to the *'sheep class'* who have symbolized their dedication to Jehovah in baptism. (*See also Bride of Christ, God's government, High Calling, Little Flock, Princes,* Remnant, *The Christ, 144,000*)

Armageddon – The Society quotes from Revelation 16:14, 16, and teaches that this *'Great War'* will begin after all religion on earth has been destroyed, and civil governments rise up against the Witnesses. God will send His armies from heaven to protect them and utterly destroy all non-Witnesses, which then ushers in the 1000 year 'Day' of Judgment. [231] (*See also Salvation*)

---

[229] **New World Translation** (Watch Tower Bible & Tract Society, 2013) Glossary of Terms

[230] Ibid, Glossary of Terms

[231] **Watch Tower Magazine** (Watch Tower Bible & Tract Society, Sept. 2012) pp. 4, 5

Atonement – The meaning of this word denotes *"at one"* which the Witnesses understand to mean being an exact equivalent to what was lost. What they believe was lost, was the *'perfect human life'* on paradise earth, which Adam and Eve forfeited by their sin. Jesus laid down his corresponding *'perfect human life'* as an exact equal (atonement) to pay the ransom price for the 144,000 first and foremost. [232] (*See also Ransom, and Perfect Human Life*)

Babylon the Great – Taken from Revelation 17:1, it is taught that Babylon the Great, the *'harlot'* represents the combined false religions of the world (every religious belief not taught by the Watch Tower Society). [233] (*See also Christendom, Religion, and Nominal Church*)

Baptism – The Witnesses believe the word *"baptize"* means to *"dip,"* and is not sprinkling or pouring, which is what the Greek word *'baptizo'* denotes. To them, water baptism signifies ones desire to have a relationship with Jehovah God. But to qualify for baptism there are several steps that must first be taken. (1) knowledge of what the Watch Tower teaches concerning Jehovah and Jesus, (2) faith in Gods' promises (According to the WTS) and the saving power of Jesus' sacrifice, (3) Taking part in the organized 'preaching' of the Jehovah's Witnesses, [door knocking] (4) Repent and reform your life, (5) make changes in your lifestyle and habits, (6)

---

[232] **You May Survive Armageddon into God's New World** (Watch Tower Bible & Tract Society, 1955) p. 39

[233] **Awake Magazine** (Watch Tower Bible & Tract Society, Nov. 2012) p. 13

Dedicate yourself to Jehovah God [Watch Tower] (7) Meet with the elders so they can determine your knowledge and dedication [about a 4 hour interview]. After these things are verified by the elders, the individual is ready to '*symbolize*' his dedication to Jehovah by being baptized. He dies to his former life course, and is raised alive to do Jehovah's will. He is now a member of God's organization – the Watch Tower Society of Jehovah's Witnesses. Baptism does not remit sin, nor is it meant as a plan for salvation. Salvation comes through being part of the WTS and faithfully preaching the rest of one's life. [234] (*See also Perfect Human Life, Preaching, Ransom, Reconciliation, and Remission of Sins*)

Bride of Christ - Jehovah's Witnesses believe Jesus is the Great Spirit who is head & king of Zion, God's capital organization, which is the kingdom, the Church of Christ. The members of the church which are the '*body of Christ*,' are also the '*bride of Christ*,' comprising Jesus and the 144,000. [235] [236] (*See also Anointed, God's government, High calling, Little Flock, Princes, Remnant, The Christ, The Church of Christ, 144,000*)

Christendom – The WTS claims they are **not part** of Christendom; nor are they part of Judaism or Islam. [237]

---

[234] **What Does the Bible Really Teach?** (Watch Tower Bible & Tract Society, 2010) pp. 174-182

[235] J.F. Rutherford, **Children** (Watch Tower Bible & Tract Society, 1941) p. 231

[236] Charles T. Russell, **The Divine Plan of the Ages** (The Dawn Bible Students Association, 1916) pp. 93, 105

[237] **How Can You Have a Happy Life?** (Watch Tower Bible & Tract Society, 2013) contents page

Witnesses believe the Catholic Church and Protestant denominations are a sham Christianity (which is true). [238] They assert there is only one Christendom, and it is a false, hypocritical religious organizations that have always been a part of Babylon the Great. [239] (*See also Babylon the Great, Deliverance, Religion, and Nominal Church*)

Cities of Refuge – The Watch Tower Society believes this term refers to a type of God's organization, namely the Watch Tower Bible and Tract Society. When one is baptized symbolically they are agreeing to obey God's will and are fleeing for refuge to God's organization. [240] [241] (*See also, Faithful and Discreet Slave, God's organization, Noah's Ark, and Zion*)

Conversion – It is taught that Christ will return before the conversion of the world. The purpose of the Millennial Day of Judgment is to convert the world to Watch Towerites. [242]

Dates

1914 – According to the Society, this year is a very important year in Bible prophecy. Witnesses believe it

---

[238] **You May Survive Armageddon into God's New World** (Watch Tower Bible & Tract, 1955) p. 208

[239] **The Nations shall Know that I am Jehovah"** (Watch Tower Bible & Tract Society, 1971) p. 206

[240] J.F. Rutherford, **Salvation** (Watch Tower Bible & Tract Society, 1939) p. 271

[241] J.F. Rutherford, **Riches** (Watch Tower Bible & Tract Society, 1936) p. 127

[242] Charles T. Russell, **The Divine Plan of the Ages** (The Dawn Bible Students Association, 1916) p. 91

marks the legal end of the Gentile times or the end of the world. It was also the year that Jehovah installed Jesus as heavenly king, and the beginning of the 'last days.' To become a Jehovah's Witness, one must confess total faith in this date. [243] [244]

1918 – After the end of the world failed to appear in 1914, Rutherford set 1918 as the end date, with the destruction of all religion and the beginning of the resurrection of the 144,000. [245] [246] (*See also Religion*)

1925 – With the failure of 1918, Rutherford began preaching meetings around the world and passing out his new booklet, *"Millions Now Living will Never Die."* He predicted that October 1925 would usher in the beginning of the end with the resurrection of Abraham, Isaac, and Jacob who would be made visible to all on earth. They believe the end of Christianity would occur, and earth would be turned into paradise for eternity. [247] [248]

---

[243] J.F. Rutherford, **Creation** (Watch Tower Bible & Tract Society, 1927) pp. 304, 307

[244] **What Does the Bible Really Teach?** (Watch Tower Bible & Tract Society, 2013) pp. 215-218

[245] **Watch Tower Magazine** (Watch Tower Bible & Tract Society, Sept. 1, 1916) p. 265

[246] Ibid, May 1, 1918, p. 132

[247] J.F. Rutherford, **Millions Now Living will Never Die** (Watch Tower Bible & Tract Society, 1918) pp. 88, 89

[248] J.F. Rutherford, **The Way to Paradise** (Watch Tower Bible & Tract Society, 1924) pp. 224, 226

1931 – This was the year Rutherford changed the name of the International Bible Students, to Jehovah's Witnesses. [249]

1935 – With the increasing numbers of *'good willed persons'* converting to the Witnesses, the doctrine concerning the 144,000 had to change. The doorway would close in this year and no more would be added to the anointed class. [250] [251] They had to add the "Other Sheep" class to cover all newcomers to the Society.

1975 – Witnesses will deny it, but between 1966 and 1975 their material implied the Battle of Armageddon would come in 1975, which would result in the end of Satan's Organization (civil governments & religion) and the ushering in of the thousand year Judgment Day. [252] [253]

Day of Jehovah – Also known as *"Jehovah's Day,"* it is believed to be the *"Great Tribulation"* (Matthew 24:21), which they say began in 1914, and which culminates in the Battle of Armageddon. [254] They are still waiting. (*See also Battle of Armageddon, and Salvation*)

---

[249] **Watch Tower Magazine** (Watch Tower Bible & Tract Society, Feb. 15, 2006) pp. 22, 23, 24, 25, 26

[250] **Jehovah's Witnesses in the Divine Purpose** (Watch Tower Bible & Tract Society, 1959) p. 140

[251] **Holy Spirit** (Watch Tower Bible & Tract Society, 1976) p. 156

[252] **Watch Tower Magazine** (Watch Tower Bible & Tract Society, Oct. 15, 1966) pp. 629, 631

[253] **Watch Tower Magazine** (Watch Tower Bible & Tract Society, Mar. 15, 1980) p. 17

[254] J.F. Rutherford, **Riches** (Watch Tower Bible & Tract Society, 1936) pp. 318, 319

Death – Jehovah's Witnesses believe death is the opposite of life. To them it means non-existence, annihilation, falsely based on the misinterpretation of Ecclesiastes 9:5, 6, 10, Psalm 146:4 and other passages. [255] (*See also Eternal Torment, Grave, Hades, Hell, Immortality, Pit, Resurrection, Sheol, and The Soul*)

Deliverance – When a person of 'good will' comes out of Satan's Organization (Babylon the Great/Religion/Christendom) and dedicates himself to serving Jehovah in God's Organization, that person is delivered. Not from sin, but from Satan's Organization. [256] (*See also Babylon the Great, Christendom, and Religion*)

Dispensations – According to the Witnesses there are three dispensations (1) The world that was, (2) This present evil world, and (3) The world to come. [257] (*See also Millennial Age*)

Demons – They say angels who became wicked are called '*demons*' in Scripture. They assert that demons have always exercised control and influence over humans to cause them to practice religion and to worship creation over the Creator. [258]

---

[255] **What Does the Bible Really Teach?** (Watch Tower Bible & Tract Society, 2013) pp. 58, 59

[256] J.F. Rutherford, **Salvation** (Watch Tower Bible & Tract Society, 1939) p. 180

[257] Charles R. Russell, The Divine Plan of the Ages (The Dawn Bible Students Association, 1916) p. 219

[258] J.F. Rutherford, **Children** (Watch Tower Bible & Tract Society, 1941) p. 64

Domestics – This term refers to the same collective body of anointed disciples (the 144,000) who are called the '*slave class*,' but the individuals of that class are highlighted in their role as '*domestics.*' [259] However, in October 2012 the Governing Body of the Watch Tower Society received '*new light*' whereby all Jehovah's Witnesses are now domestics. (*See also Anointed, Cities of Refuge, Faithful and Discreet Slave, Noah's Ark, New Light, and Zion*)

Due Time – According to the Witnesses, this refers to God's eternal purpose for mankind. Taken from 1 Timothy 2:6, where Paul states, "*who gave himself a ransom for all, to be testified in due time,*" they contend that God established a particular time (due time) for men to hear the gospel. It is now God's due time for the 144,000, but God's due time for all others is after the Battle of Armageddon, during the 1,000 year Day of Judgment. [260]

Eternal Torment – According to their teachings, eternal torment does not exist because they do not believe in an immortal soul, therefore, all who die cease to exist. Everyone's nature is stored in God's memory banks for future cloning at the resurrection. (*See also Grave, Hell, Hades, Pit, Sheol, Resurrection, Immortality, the Soul*)

---

[259] **Watch Tower Magazine** (Watch Tower Bible & Tract Society, June 15, 2009) pp. 20, 21

[260] Charles T. Russell, **The Divine Plan of the Ages** (The Dawn Bible Students Association, 1916), pp. 105, 107, 108, 113-114

Faith – Witnesses believe this word means *"To have knowledge of God's purpose as set forth in his Word, the Bible, and then to confidently rely upon God's Word of truth as therein made known by the Watch Tower Society."* [261]

Faithful and Discreet Slave – Misinterpreted from Jesus' teaching found in Matthew 24:45-47; which Jehovah's Witnesses use as their foundational Scripture for existing. They believe that in 1919 God anointed leaders for the Watch Tower Society, and charged them with being the sole source of truth. [262] From 1919 to 2009 this *'slave class'* included only *"anointed"* Witnesses, but was changed to represent the Governing Body alone in 2012. New light has now caused a retraction of their appointment, saying they are no longer appointed over all Jesus' belongings. [263] (*See also Domestics, Cities of Refuge, God's Organization, In the Truth, Noah's Ark, Zion, and 144,000*)

Gentile Time – The Witnesses believe that God's organization began with Adam in the Garden, but ceased when Adam was removed. The organization was re-established as a *'type'* when God made a covenant with the Israelites. When God removed His organization under Zedekiah it would not be re-established until the second advent of Christ in 1914. From Zedekiah until 1914 the Gentile

---

[261] J.F. Rutherford, **Salvation** (Watch Tower Bible & Tract Society, 1939) p. 33

[262] **128th Annual Meeting Report** of the Watch Tower Bible & Tract Society of Pennsylvania, October 6, 2012

[263] **Watch Tower Magazine** (Watch Tower Bible & Tract Society, July 15, 2013) pp. 22, 25

kingdoms were allowed to reign until the Day of Jehovah would begin to set up Christ's kingdom and end the *'Times of the Gentiles.'* (Luke 21:24). [264] *(See also Day of Jehovah)*

Gehenna – The Greek word *"Gehenna"* which is a reference from the Hebrew Scriptures concerning the *"Valley of Hinnom."* Hinnom was located outside the gates of Jerusalem where fires burned day and night. Witnesses believe it is not a literal place, but has a figurative meaning that denotes everlasting destruction, or complete annihilation with no hope of resurrection. They argue this is where the *'goats'* [Babylon the Great] will be cast (Matthew 25:46). [265] *(See also Babylon the Great, Hades, Hell, Grave, and Pit)* [Note: Witnesses say the goats will not be resurrected, yet they teach there will be a resurrection of the righteous and unrighteous (Acts 24:15), which is it?] [266]

Gibeonite Class – The Witnesses believe the Gibeonites were menial temple servants (Joshua 9:16-27). They look to the Old Testament for types and anti-types of which this is just one. They assert that the *'Great Multitude'* is of the *'Gibeonite Class'* who have publicly dedicated themselves by faith in Jehovah and the WTS to become humble slaves and preach

---

[264] Charles T. Russell, **The Divine Plan of the Ages** (The Dawn Bible Students Association, 1916) pp. 248, 249, 250

[265] **Let God be True** (Watch Tower Bible & Tract Society, 1946) pg. 95, 96, 97

[266] **What Does the Bible Really Teach?** (Watch Tower Bible & Tract Society, 2010) p. 213

the good news. [267] They have now declassified the *'Great Crowd'* as an unknown entity that will be known only after Armageddon. *(See also Jonadab Class, Preaching, Remnant, Other Sheep, and New Light)*

God – The Witnesses believe God is eternal and is alone the creator. God is one, meaning He does not possess three persons. God the Father is the only true God, who has given himself a name – Jehovah. He is also referred to as *"The Almighty."* [268] *(See also Jehovah)*

God's Government – They teach this government consists of Jesus, the head of God's capital organization called *'Zion,'* together with 144,000 associates (The Christ), who are designated as kings and priests unto God and Christ. All of which are spirits in the likeness of Jesus. The kingdom or government of peace is The Theocracy. [269] *(See also Anointed, Cities of Refuge, God's Government, Noah's Ark, Zion, and 144,000)*

Gospel Age - It is believed that this is the *'trial-day'* for life or death for those called to the Divine nature. [270] Even though the gospel is not to be preached at this time, this represents the time when the anointed (the 144,000), are being tested

---

[267] **You May Survive Armageddon into God's New World** (Watch Tower Bible & Tract Society, 1955), p. 241

[268] **What Does the Bible Really Teach?** (Watch Tower Bible & Tract Society, 2013) pp. 14-15

[269] J.F. Rutherford, **Salvation** (Watch Tower Bible & Tract Society, 1939) p. 307

[270] Charles T. Russell, **The Divine Plan of the Ages** (The Dawn Bible Students Association, 1916) p. 141

since Jesus' rise to kinghood in 1914. These 'slaves' are being proved for their fitness to become members of 'the Christ' at the end of the gospel age. [271]

Grave – By their way of thinking, the Witnesses define the Greek word '*Hades*,' as '*death*.' They believe it is the common grave of the dead, a figurative location for those who '*sleep in death*,' or non-existence. This is the sort of death [non-existence] from which there will be a resurrection. [272] (*See also Death, Eternal Torment, Hell, Hades, Immortality, Pit, Resurrection, Sheol, and the Soul*)

Great Multitude - According to Watch Tower teaching, the majority of Jehovah's Witnesses make up what they call the '*Great Multitude*,' or the '*Other Sheep*.' These are the Witnesses that will inherit Paradise Earth forever while the 144,000 anointed '*class*' will rule over them from heaven. [273] [274] In 2012, this doctrine received '*new light*' and now all Witnesses will receive heaven. They are now unsure who will live on paradise earth. They have now declassified the '*Great Crowd*' as an unknown entity that will be known only after Armageddon. (*See also Gibeonite Class, Jonadab Class, Other Sheep, and New Light*)

---

[271] Ibid, p. 231

[272] **What Does the Bible Really Teach?** (Watch Tower Bible & Tract Society, 2010) pp. 212, 213

[273] **You May Survive Armageddon into God's New World** (Watch Tower Bible & Tract Society, 1955) pp. 46, 226, 314

[274] **Man's Salvation out of World Distress at Hand!** (Watch Tower Bible & Tract Society, 1975) pp. 170, 201, 202

Hades – From the Greek word '*Hades*,' the Watch Tower renders it as '*death*.' They believe it is the common grave of the dead, a figurative location for those who '*sleep in death*,' or non-existence. This is the sort of death [non-existence] from which there will be resurrection. [275] (*See also Eternal Torment, Grave, Hell, Immortality, Pit, Resurrection, Sheol and the Soul*)

Heaven – Believed to be where Jehovah God, Jesus and the angels dwell (which is true). They say it is headquarters for God's invisible organization and where Jesus and the 144,000 will reign forever over the visible kingdom on paradise earth. Only the 144,000 will see Jehovah and Jesus, and will enjoy a heavenly home. [276] In 2012, this doctrine received '*new light*' which now teaches that all Witnesses will receive heaven. They are now unsure who will live on paradise earth and comprise the Great Crowd class. (*See also God's Organization, and Faithful and Discreet Slave, New Light*)

Hell – Because the King James Version renders the Hebrew word "*Sheol*" and the Greek word "*Hades*" as "*hell*," "*grave*," and "*pit*," the Witnesses have irrationally used this to further their doctrine of annihilation. They assert that each of these words means "*mankind's common grave or pit of burial*." [277]

---

[275] **What Does the Bible Really Teach?** (Watch Tower Bible & Tract Society, 2010) pp. 212, 213

[276] **Jehovah's Witnesses – Proclaimers of God's Kingdom** (Watch Tower Bible & Tract Society, 1993) pp. 159, 164, 169

[277] **What Does the Bible Really Teach?** (Watch Tower Bible & Tract Society, 2010) pp. 89, 90

(See also Death, Eternal Torment, Grave, Hades, Immortality, Pit, Resurrection, Sheol, and the Soul)

High Calling – They believe this refers to Jehovah's invitation for all true Christians (JW's) of this age to become joint-heirs with Christ and partakers of the divine nature. This 'High Calling' however does not apply to all Witnesses, only the anointed class are able to receive it. This invitation ceased however after 1935 when the number of Witnesses grew well over the 144,000 number, thereby granting all others eternal life on earth. [278] *(See also Anointed, God's Government, Little Flock, Princes, Other Sheep, Remnant, and 144,000)*

Holy Spirit – Witnesses believe Jehovah God is not a *'trinity,'* and the general thought that the *"Holy Spirit"* is the third person of the 'trinity' and equal with God and Christ is spurious. They assert that the Holy Spirit is the invisible active force of Almighty God which moves his servants to do his will. [279] *(See also The Trinity)*

Immortality – The immortality of the soul is a doctrine not accepted by the Jehovah's Witnesses. Because of their belief that death means non-existence, they cannot accept an immortal soul since that would deny annihilation. Witnesses believe that only Jehovah God is immortal, and that Jesus gained immortality after His resurrection. Since God is

---

[278] Charles T. Russell, **The Time is at Hand** (Watch Tower Bible & Tract Society, 1916) p. 235
[279] **Let God be True** (Watch Tower Bible & Tract Society, 1946) pp. 107, 108

inherently immortal, Witnesses must eat of the Tree of Life to stay alive on paradise earth. [280] [281]

"In the Truth" – It is taught and believed that all truth comes from God through the Watch Tower Society, therefore only Jehovah's Witnesses are *'in the truth.'* [282] (*See also Faithful and Discreet Slave*)

Incarnation – The incarnation of Jesus is false according to the Witnesses. Since they do not believe Jesus is God, but a created spirit being also referred to as *"Michael the Archangel,"* they declare that God through His electric force (Holy Spirit) impregnated Mary by changing or transmuting the spirit being Michael into the human-being Jesus (his earthly name). Jesus had to be 100% human in order to regain the *'perfect human life'* Adam lost when he sinned. [283] [284] (*See also Michael the Archangel, Perfect Human Life*)

Jehovah – All Adventists (From which the JW's are just one of many branches) believe Jehovah to be the personal name applied to God the Father as the Supreme Being which is to be

---

[280] J.F. Rutherford, **Reconciliation** (Watch Tower Bible & Tract Society, 1928) pp. 75, 76, 77, 78, 79

[281] **What Does the Bible Really Teach?** (Watch Tower Bible & Tract Society, 2010) pp. 208, 209, 210, 211

[282] **Watch Tower Magazine** (Watch Tower Bible & Tract Society, June 1, 1985) p. 30

[283] Charles T. Russell, **Studies in the Scriptures, Vol. V, Study III** (Watch Tower Bible & Tract Society, 1916) pp. 94, 95, 96

[284] **Watch Tower Magazine** (Watch Tower Bible & Tract Society, June 15, 1998) p. 22

treated as sacred. [285] (*See also God and Appendix p. 179*).

Jehovah's Witnesses

True Followers – Jehovah's Witnesses are the only true followers of God, following in the steps of Paul, Peter, John the Baptist, Moses, Abraham, Noah and Abel who were themselves Witnesses. Each Witness is an anointed minister of the gospel; preaching the good news of eternal life on paradise earth, and defending God's true name – Jehovah. [286]

Jesus – They believe He is Jehovah's most precious Son because God created him first (Colossians 1:15). It is believed He is the "*only begotten Son*" because He was the only one directly created by God (John 3:16). God then used Jesus to create all other things (Colossians 1:16). [287]

Jonadab Class – Jehovah's Witnesses believe the '*Great Crowd*' are of the Jonadab class (2 Kings 10:15-28). These are people who stand on the side of righteousness and against Satan's organization (Christendom), and who alone will be preserved at Armageddon. [288] They have now declassified the '*Great Crowd*' as an unknown entity that will be known only

---

[285] **Jehovah's Witnesses – Proclaimers of God's Kingdom** (Watch Tower Bible & Tract Society, 1993) pp. 123, 124

[286] **Let God be True** (Watch Tower Bible & Tract Society, 1946) pp. 222, 224, 226

[287] **What Does the Bible Really Teach?** (Watch Tower Bible & Tract Society, 2010) p. 41

[288] **Jehovah's Witnesses – Proclaimers of God's Kingdom** (Watch Tower Bible & Tract Society, 1993) p. 165

after Armageddon. *(See also Gibeonite Class, Jonadab Class, Other Sheep, and Remnant)*

Judgment Day – They assert this is not one day, but a period of one thousand years, as trillions of people could not possibly be judged in one day. Its purpose will be to judge inhabited earth in righteousness, after the Battle of Armageddon has cleansed the earth of its wicked inhabitants. Judgment is really a test to see if one is worthy of eternal life on earth. All Witnesses from Abel, to those alive when Armageddon comes will be tested during the Millennial reign of 'The Christ' (Jesus + 144,000). [289] *(See also Resurrection)*

Justification – Denotes being made right with God. The 144,000 living in the Christian era are justified by faith in the shed blood of Jesus, while the *'great multitude'* will be justified after Armageddon by their works. Their justification will result in being given the right to live as human creatures on paradise earth. [290] [291] In 2012, this doctrine received *'new light'* and now all Witnesses will receive heaven. They are now unsure who will live on paradise earth. *(See also New Light)*

Little Flock – The Witnesses believe this is the only class who are *'born again.'* God has chosen them out of all nations

---

[289] Ibid, pp. 284, 286, 288, 289
[290] J.F. Rutherford, **Reconciliation** (Watch Tower Bible & Tract Society, 1928) pp. 164, 169
[291] J.F. Rutherford, **Riches** (Watch Tower Bible & Tract Society, 1936) p. 44

to rule in heaven with Jesus as '*the Christ*.' [292] They comprise 144,000 kingdom heirs whom God anointed to represent Him here on earth before being resurrected to heaven. [293] (*See also Anointed, 144,000, The Christ, God's government, high calling, Little Flock, Princes, and Remnant*)

Mediator – The Witnesses have a slanted view of the Mediatorship of Jesus that teaches Jesus is only mediator between Jehovah and spiritual Israel (the 144,000). [294] His being mediator was the giving of His perfect human life in exchange for the perfect human life Adam lost when he sinned; thereby removing inherited sin from the little flock. [295] [296]

Michael the Archangel – Witnesses believe Scripture teaches Michael defended Jehovah's rulership and fought His enemies, therefore living up to his name "*Who is Like God?*" They believe the Bible indicates that Michael is the spiritual name of the Logos, while Jesus is His physical name. Jesus will return as Michael to fight the Battle of Armageddon. [297] [298] (*See also Incarnation & Appendix p. 202*)

---

[292] **Jehovah's Witnesses – Proclaimers of God's Kingdom** (Watch Tower Bible & Tract Society, 1993) p. 145

[293] Ibid, pp. 159, 162

[294] **Worldwide Security Under the Prince of Peace** (Watchtower Bible & Tract Society) pp. 10, 11

[295] J.F. Rutherford, **Salvation** (Watch Tower Bible & Tract Society, 1939) p. 180

[296] **Watch Tower Magazine** (Watch Tower Bible & Tract Society, Nov. 15, 1979) p. 27

[297] **What Does the Bible Really Teach?** (Watch Tower Bible & Tract Society, 2010) pp. 218, 219

[298] **Watch Tower Magazine** (Watch Tower Bible & Tract Society, May 15, 1969) p. 307

Millennial Age – The Watch Tower believes this is the time following Armageddon, when the church will be established so Jesus and the 144,000 can reign from heaven over the earthly kingdom. It will be a time of teaching when the gospel will be taught for the first time and everyone resurrected (cloned) will be required to learn of God's ways or be destroyed in the *'second death.'* [299] [300] (*See also Judgment Day*)

Ministration of Angels – They teach this is the first dispensation from creation to the flood when God allowed angels to try and recover fallen man. But the degeneration of mankind caused God's wrath to be initiated through the flood and the second dispensation *"present evil world,"* was established. (They cite Hebrews 2:5) [301] (*See also Dispensations*)

New Light – Referred to by the Witnesses as *"Increasing Light"* this concept is gleaned from Proverbs 4:18 and Daniel 12:4. It is their belief that God provides them (WTS) with progressive understanding of the Scriptures, through changes in prophecy. Yet that does not harmonize with God's word who said we can know if God is behind the prophecy or not (Deuteronomy 18). This stance offers them the ability to continually tweak their beliefs while asserting it does not

---

[299] **Your Will be Done on Earth** (Watch Tower Bible & Tract Society, 1958) p. 354

[300] **Revelation – It's Grand Climax at Hand!** (Watch Tower Bible & Tract Society, 1988) p. 6

[301] Charles T. Russell, **The Divine Plan of the Ages** (The Dawn Bible Students Association, 1916) p. 220

mean they are teaching error. [302] The fact of the matter is that God's word is His final revelation to all men and women (Jude 3; 1 Corinthians 13:10-12). [NOTE: The World-Wide Church of God, Christadelphians, Adventists, Mormons, Quakers, Pentecostals and Catholics hold this same belief] (*See also Domestics, God's Government, Heaven and Appendix p. 175*)

New Heaven - This phrase refers to '*new rule*' in heaven over the earth. The present 'heavens' are made up of man-made governments, but they will be replaced after Armageddon by God's heavenly government made up of Jesus and the 144,000 or 'The Christ.' [303]

New Earth – What is this? Witnesses say it is not a new planet because God created this earth to remain forever (Psalm 104:5). The '*New Earth*' means a new society of people because the Bible often uses the word '*Earth*' to mean people. The Earth that will be destroyed is the people who have attached themselves to the '*wicked system of things*,' like civil governments and religion. [304] (*See also Babylon the Great, Christendom, Nominal Church, and Religion*)

Noah's Ark – Witnesses believe this refers to a type of God's organization - the Watch Tower Society. When one is baptized symbolically they are agreeing to obey God's will and are

---

[302] **Watch Tower Magazine** "Study Edition," (Watch Tower Bible & Tract Society, July 15, 2013)

[303] **You Can Live Forever in Paradise Earth** (Watch Tower Bible & Tract Society, 1982) p. 160

[304] Ibid, p. 160

fleeing for refuge to God's organization. [305] (*See also Cities of Refuge, Faithful and Discreet Slave, God's Organization, and Zion*)

Nominal church – This refers to all the churches of Christendom with all their unscriptural doctrines and divisions. It refers to those not really converted for only Jehovah's Witnesses are the one true church of Christ). [306] [307] (*See also Babylon the Great, Christendom, and Religion*)

Old Light – Truth is truth, it does not progress as the Witnesses assume. They claim Jehovah directly reveals truth to them through the Watch Tower Society, but that He does so progressively, refining previous truth. [308] There is a difference between refinement and complete change which is common with their doctrines. It is past doctrine that they refer to as "*old light.*"

Other Sheep – Taken from John 10:16, Witnesses apply it to those other than the '*Little Flock*' (144,000). At one time it referred to the '*Great Crowd*' class of Witnesses who will inherit paradise earth; those not among the household of God or body of Christ. However, '*new light*' has been given concerning this class of Witnesses, which now sets them equal

---

[305] J.F. Rutherford, **Salvation** (Watch Tower Bible & Tract Society, 1939) p. 271

[306] Charles T. Russell, **The Divine Plan of the Ages** (The Dawn Bible Students Association, 1916) p. 287

[307] **Jehovah's Witnesses – Proclaimers of God's Kingdom** (Watch Tower Bible & Tract Society, 1993) p. 160

[308] **Watch Tower Magazine** (Watch Tower Bible & Tract Society, May 15, 2011) p. 27

with the anointed class (144,000). They have now declassified the 'Great Crowd' as an unknown entity that will be known only after Armageddon [309]. It would appear the Faithful Slave was correct the first time, before 'new light' caused them to divide themselves into two classes. (*See also Gibeonite Class, Jonadab Class, and Remnant*)

Paradise – This is a reference to earth being returned to the Garden of Eden. It is never a reference to heaven or hades. They assert that Jesus told the thief that he would live on paradise earth. [310]

Peculiar People – It is their belief that God has called the 'Little Flock' to walk a peculiar course, which is why they are referred to as a 'peculiar people.' (*See also Anointed, Little Flock, Remnant, The Christ, and 144,000*)

Perfect Human Life – According to the Witnesses this is what was lost in the Garden of Eden when Adam sinned. Therefore, this is what Jesus's sacrifice consisted of in order for the anointed class to inherit the divine nature in heaven, and the remnant to inherit paradise earth. [311] The goal is to obtain a perfect human life to inherit paradise earth. (*See also Baptism, Ransom, and Remission of Sins*)

---

[309] **128ᵗʰ Annual Meeting Report** of the Watch Tower Bible & Tract Society of Pennsylvania, October 6, 2012

[310] J.F. Rutherford, **Riches** (Watch Tower Bible & Tracts Society, 1936) pp. 182, 183

[311] **Let God be True** (Watch Tower Bible & Tract Society, 1946) p. 114

Pit – Falsely taken from the King James Version that exchanges different English words for the Greek word '*Hades.*' They believe it is the common grave of the dead, a figurative location for those who '*sleep in death,*' or non-existence. This is the sort of death [non-existence] from which there will be resurrection. [312] (*See also Death, Eternal Torment, Grave, Hell, Hades, Immortality, Resurrection, Sheol, and the Soul*)

Preaching – Also referred to as '*Field Ministry,*' the Witnesses understand every member to be an ordained minister with the command to go out into the entire world and preach. They do this through door to door distribution of materials such as Watch Tower and Awake Magazines and setting up one on one studies of their material. Hours devoted to preaching depends largely upon one's dedication and what the elders require of each publisher, pioneer, special pioneer, etc. [313] (*See also Baptism, and Gibeonite Class*)

"Twelve Reasons for Preaching
1. It helps save lives. ...
2. It serves to warn the wicked
3. It contributes to the fulfillment of Bible prophecy
4. It is an expression of God's righteousness
5. It allows us to discharge our debt...
6. It enables us to avoid bloodguilt
7. It is a requirement for our own salvation."

---

[312] **What Does the Bible Really Teach?** (Watch Tower Bible & Tract Society, 2010) pp. 212, 213

[313] **Jehovah's Witnesses – Proclaimers of God's Kingdom** (Watch Tower Bible & Tract Society, 1993) pp. 82, 301, 717 et al

8. It demonstrates love for neighbor
9. It shows obedience to Jehovah and his Son
10. It is part of our worship
11. It expresses our love for God
12. It contributes toward the sanctification of Jehovah's name

Kingdom Ministry 2012 Jun p.1 (US Edition)

Princes – Also referred to as the Royal House, the Royal Priesthood, the Kingdom Class, the Elect, the Holy Nation, Israel of God, Spiritual Israel, Spirit Begotten, Sanctuary Class, Sons of Levi, Chosen Ones, these are the Little Flock who are limited to the number 144,000. (*See also Anointed, Faithful and Discreet Slave, God's government, High Calling, Little Flock, Princes, Remnant, The Christ, The Church of Christ, and Zion*)

Ransom – It is maintained that a perfect human life on paradise earth for eternity was God's original plan when He set Adam and Eve in the Garden. However, a perfect human life was lost when Adam sinned, therefore a '*corresponding ransom*' (perfect human life) had to be given so mankind could gain back what was lost. [314] This ransom price applies only to the anointed class in the immediate sense, and to all others in the potential sense. (*See also Baptism, Perfect Human Life, Reconciliation, and Remission of Sins*)

---

[314] **What Does the Bible Really Teach?** (Watch Tower Bible & Tract Society, 2010) pp. 48, 49, 50

Reconciliation - Because of the *'ransom'* price paid by Jesus, God is able to *'reconcile'* certain anointed ones and add them to His organization, the body of Christ. Because the *'other sheep'* are not born again and not in the new covenant as are the 144,000, they must work their way to justification by preaching, living a pure life, and passing the thousand year Judgment Day test. [315] (*See also Perfect Human Life, Ransom, and Remission of Sins*)

Religion – It is believed that there is no such thing as religion or Christian religion because they argue that Christianity is not a religion. To the Witnesses, religion is synonymous with Babylon the Great. [316] (*See also Babylon the Great, Christendom, Deliverance, and Nominal Church*)

Remission of Sins – Baptism does not remit sin, but only symbolizes one's desire to dedicate their lives to Jehovah's service. Jesus' ransom was paid for the 144,000, only they have their inherited sins remitted by His perfect human life, and are made sons of God. The Other Sheep must work their way to salvation (remission of sins, which means remission of inherited sin). [317] [318](*See also Baptism, Other Sheep, Perfect Human Life, Ransom, and Reconciliation*)

---

[315] J.F. Rutherford, **Reconciliation** (Watch Tower Bible & Tract Society, 1928) pp. 253, 254, 247, 335

[316] J.F. Rutherford, **Government** (Watch Tower Bible & Tract Society, 1928) pp. 138, 139

[317] **The Truth that Leads to Eternal Life** (Watch Tower Bible & Tract Society, 1968) pp. 106, 107

[318] **What Does the Bible Really Teach?** (Watch Tower Bible & Tract Society, 2010) pp. 48, 49, 50

Remnant – Witnesses believe there are two remnant classes (1) Priestly Remnant, and (2) Jeremiah Remnant. The Jeremiah remnant comes from the *'other sheep'* class who survive Armageddon, while the Priestly remnant is spiritual Israel, the body of Christ, the 144,000. The Priestly remnant refers to God's Organization – the Faithful and Discreet Slave. [319] [320] [321] (*See also, Faithful and Discreet Slave, Gibeonite Class, God's Organization, Jonadab Class, and Other Sheep*)

Restitution – The Watch Tower teaches that God's plan since Adam's condemnation is a restoration or restitution of mankind to human perfection on paradise earth (Acts 3:21). [322] (*See also Perfect Human Life*)

Resurrection – Witnesses allege that the pagan doctrine of the *"inherent immortality of the human soul"* was introduced and adopted into the apostate *"Christian"* organization. Belief in that teaching wrecked man's true Christian faith, because it set at naught the Scriptural truth that at death the human soul (the entire person) goes to the grave (non-existence – Ecclesiastes 9:10). There are two resurrections (1) the *'first'* resurrection is for the 'little flock' being limited to the 144,000; (2) the *'earthly'* resurrection is for the greater mass of humankind and *'other sheep'* who will inherit paradise

---

[319] **You May Survive Armageddon into God's New World** (Watch Tower Bible & Tract Society, 1955) pp. 62, 63

[320] **Jehovah's Witnesses – Proclaimers of God's Kingdom** (Watch Tower Bible & Tract Society, 1993) pp. 146, 218, 219

[321] J.F. Rutherford, **Salvation** (Watch Tower Bible & Tract Society, 1939) p. 60

[322] Charles T. Russell, **The Divine Plan of the Ages** (The Dawn Bible Students Association, 1916) p. 149

earth. In reality it is a *'recreation'* as our existing bodies turn back to dust and God must clone us from His memory. [323] [324] *(See also Death, Eternal Torment, Grave, Hell, Hades, Immortality, Pit, Sheol, and the Soul)*

Salvation – To the Jehovah's Witness, salvation does not the same meaning as the majority or people understand the word. The Witnesses believe it denotes *"Deliverance from impending disaster, and finding refuge in a place of complete safety."* [325] While this definition is true, they do not believe it refers to deliverance from eternity in hell, but deliverance from the Battle of Armageddon. The place of safety refers to the Watch Tower Society - God's Organization. [326] *(See also Armageddon and Appendix p. 189)*

Sheol – According to Watch Tower doctrine, the Hebrew word *'Sheol'* and the Greek word *'Hades'* are synonymous for death. They believe it is not a literal place, but figurative language for where mankind sleeps in death. It is man's common grave where we cease to exist. [327] [328] *(See also Death, Eternal Torment, Grave, Hell, Hades, Immortality, Pit, Resurrection, and the Soul)*

---

[323] **Let God be True** (Watch Tower Bible & Tract Society, 1946), pp. 277, 279, 280

[324] **The Truth that Leads to Eternal Life** (Watch Tower Bible & Tract Society, 1968) p. 110

[325] J.F. Rutherford, **Salvation** (Watch Tower Bible & Tract Society, 1939) p. 10

[326] Ibid, p. 301

[327] **Let God be True** (Watch Tower Bible & Tract Society, 1946) p. 90

[328] **What Does the Bible Really Teach?** (Watch Tower Bible & Tract Society, 2010) pp. 212, 213

Spiritual Israel – Witnesses believe this is the church, the kingdom of God, and they would be correct. However, they assert that it comprises Jesus and the 144,000 in heaven, which is incorrect. (*See also Little Flock, Remnant, The Christ, The Church of Christ, The Kingdom, and 144,000*)

Strange Work – Believed to be a work of God done only through the Watch Tower Organization, they suggest others find their work strange because they proclaim God's name as '*Jehovah.*' They believe that religion is of the devil, and that salvation is only available through God's organization – the Watch Tower Society. God will end this work shortly before Armageddon. [329]

The Christ – One doctrine that is different than what most Christians understand, is that concerning the Christ. Through manipulating various Scriptures, they assert the 'seed' promise as given to Abraham (Genesis 12:1-3) is a reference to '*the Christ,*' head and body, Jesus and the 144,000. [330] This body in heaven will dispense all spiritual blessings (reconciliation and restitution) upon the immortal clones on earth. They allege that the promise given to Abraham has not yet been fulfilled and cannot be fulfilled until the promises concerning the '*the Christ*' (head and body) are completed. [331]

---

[329] J.F. Rutherford, **Salvation** (Watch Tower Bible & Tract Society, 1939) pp. 23, 24, 58, 59, 127

[330] J.F. Rutherford, **Reconciliation** (Watch Tower Bible & Tract Society, 1928) pp. 161-164, 169

[331] Charles T. Russell, **The Divine Plan of the Ages** (The Dawn Bible Students Association, 1916) pp. 81, 82, 293, 300

(See also Anointed, God's Government, Remnant, and 144,000)

The Church of Christ – Believed to be only the class whose names are written in heaven (the 144,000). [332] *(See also Anointed, Bride of Christ, Little Flock, Princes, The Christ, The Church of Christ, and 144,000)*

The Evening Meal - Known to others as *"The Lord's Supper,"* or *"Communion,"* Witnesses refer to it as *"The Lord's Evening Meal."* Every Passover, Witnesses use this as an opportunity for *'preaching,'* by handing out special invitations to this event, as well as to hear a special *'talk'* on Sunday. After sunset on Passover (Thursday before Easter) Witnesses gather to observe the memorial of Jesus' death. After hearing a talk about the memorial prayers are said for the bread and the wine, then the loaf of unleavened bread is passed around the room, followed by the red wine. However, only those who have entered into the new covenant with Jehovah are allowed to partake of the emblems which are the 144,000. All others are only respectful observers, since Jesus only shed His blood for the anointed. [333] *(See also Appendix p. 214)*

The First Resurrection – First in time of occurrence, in quality and in importance and limited to the *"Little Flock"* or

---

[332] Ibid, p. 308
[333] **What Does the Bible Really Teach?** (Watch Tower Bible & Tract Society, 2010) pp. 206. 207

the 144,000. [334]

The Gospel – To the Witnesses, preaching the '*gospel*' is how they work their way to being saved after Armageddon and the establishment of the millennial kingdom. Their idea of '*good news*' is that Jehovah has established a two-fold kingdom (heavenly and earthly) which is also referred to as God's Government/Organization. Since heaven is already filled with the 144,000, all anyone else can hope for, is earthly paradise as a clone. However, with the advent of '*new light*' which continues to be refined, it appears that all Witnesses will now receive a heavenly home. [335] [336] (*See also Other Sheep*)

The King's Highway – Taken from Isaiah 35:8, the Witnesses believe after Armageddon, at the beginning of the 1,000 year Day of Judgment, all cloned sinners will stand at the entrance of the highway that leads to eternal life. Abraham, Isaac and Jacob will provide them instructions concerning the new covenant and its statutory laws that lead the way to reconciliation. However, these sinners must cleanse themselves in holiness before being allowed to walk on the highway. But before the highway is opened, the devil must be bound. Even though a person has wickedly told lies about the Watch Tower Society, he may through 'The Christ' turn from

---

[334] **Let God be True** (Watch Tower Bible & Tract Society, 1946) p. 277

[335] J.F. Rutherford, **Salvation** (Watch Tower Bible & Tract Society, 1939) p. 21

[336] **128th Annual Meeting Report** of the Watch Tower Bible & Tract Society of Pennsylvania, October 6, 2012

his wicked ways and be permitted to walk the highway. 337

The Lord's Day – According to the Witnesses the Lord's Day is not one particular day, but a series of days beginning with the year 1914. It refers to Christ beginning his reign on the throne of David, also referred to as the Day of Jehovah, and the Day of the Lord. They do not believe it is Sunday, the '*day*' when Christians assemble to remember the Lord's death. 338

The Meek – This term according to the Witnesses refers to those individuals who are desirous to learn WT doctrine/truth (Luke 2:911). 339

The New Creation – This is another term used to refer to "*the Christ.*" It is taught that the anointed members of the body being numbered 144,000, no more, and no less, when completed will bear the name and nature of the Eternal Father. 340

The Second Death – After the 1,000 year Day of Judgment, all Witnesses that have yielded to Satan's last ditch effort of temptations will be judged unworthy of eternal life and put to death – the '*second death*' which is symbolized by the phrase '*Lake of Fire.*' All such individuals will then be wiped from

---

337 J.F. Rutherford, **Reconciliation** (Watch Tower Bible & Tract Society, 1928), pp. 313-329

338 Charles T. Russell, **The Divine Plan of the Ages** (The Dawn Bible Students Association, 1916) pp. 307-342

339 J.F. Rutherford, **Creation** (Watch Tower Bible & Tract Society, 1927) p. 324

340 Ibid, pp. 319, 321, 324, 326

God's memory banks once and for all time. [341] [342]

The Seed – Through poor hermeneutics, Witnesses have melded several terms never meant to portray the same idea, but in their minds they do. The seed which refers to Jesus Christ (Genesis 3:15; Galatians 3:16) is believed to constitute *'the Christ'* which they say is also the Great Deliver and the Church. Each of these terms relates to Jesus and the 144,000 who together will bless the world. [343] The extent to which they twist the Scriptures is amazing. Read how Mr. Rutherford explains the seeds purpose.

> *"One of the parables taught by Jesus bears upon this same matter. A parable is a symbolic or figurative statement that pictures some reality. Jesus spoke a parable concerning a certain rich man called Dives and a beggar named Lazarus, (Luke 16:19-31). Dives, meaning rich man, represented the Jewish people who had received the special favor of Jehovah God. Lazarus pictured the non-Jews who had received no favor, therefore were in the attitude of beggars. "And it came to pass, that the beggar died, and was carried by the angels into Abraham's bosom: the rich man also died, and was buried; and in hell he lift up his eyes, being in torments, and seeth Abraham afar*

---

[341] **Then is Finished the Mystery of God** (Watch Tower Bible & Tract Society, 1969) pp. 125-127

[342] **Let God be True** (Watch Tower Bible & Tract Society, 1946), p. 293

[343] Charles T. Russell, **The Divine Plan of the Ages** (The Dawn Bible Students Association, 1916) p. 82

off, and Lazarus in his bosom." (Luke 16:22-23).

The dying of Dives and Lazarus represents a complete change of their respective conditions. Abraham, being a representative of the Lord, pictured God; Abraham's bosom figuratively represented the place of God's favor. God through Christ cast the Jews away, thereby completely withdrawing favor from them. the Gentiles or non-Jews then in due time were brought into the favor of God, and during the Christian era these have had the privilege of becoming members of the 'seed' according to the promise made to Abraham. Those who have thus been brought into God's favor and who have proven faithful to their privileges of serving the Lord will in due time have a part in the work of reconciliation with God will do through Christ for the benefit of mankind." [344]

Though not clear in his statements, '*Christ*,' always refers to '*the Christ*,' head and body, Jesus and the 144,000. The Christ, and the 'seed,' are one and the same body. *(See also Anointed, Bride of Christ, Little Flock, Peculiar People, Remnant, The Christ, The church of Christ, 144,000)*

The Soul – According to the Witnesses, there is no such thing as an eternal soul that is separate and apart from flesh

---

[344] J.F. Rutherford, **Reconciliation** (Watch Tower Bible & Tract Society, 1928) pp. 175-176

and blood. They assert that every person is '*a*' soul, and that the word simply means one's life as a person. [345] (*See also Death, Eternal Torment, Grave, Hell, Hades, Immortality, Pit, Resurrection, and Sheol*)

The Trinity – According to Watch Tower teaching it is alleged that the doctrine of the Trinity is traced back to the ancient Babylonians and Egyptians and other ancient mythologists, that the Godhead are three persons, the Father, the Son and the Holy Spirit. God's justice would not let Jesus, as a ransom, be more than a perfect man. So he could not be the supreme God Almighty in the flesh. [346] (*See also Holy Spirit, God, and Jesus*)

Zion – The Society teaches that 'Zion' is one of God's designations for His organization – The Watch Tower Bible and Tract Society. [347] (*See also Cities of Refuge, God's Government, and Noah's Ark*)

144,000 – Teachings on this number have changed over the years as they continually receive '*new light*.' In the beginning, when this sect first began, it referred to all of Russell's Bible Students, but when Rutherford realized their numbers were increasing, he changed it to a select few, and created the "Great Crowd" class to cover the remainder of the Witnesses.

---

[345] **What Does the Bible Really Teach?** (Watch Tower Bible & Tract Society, 2010) pp. 208. 209

[346] **Let God be True** (Watch Tower Bible & Tract Society, 1946), pp. 100, 101, 106

[347] J.F. Rutherford, **Prophecy** (Watch Tower Bible & Tract Society, 1929), p. 83

This group alone is Jehovah's saved class, the Christ, the church, His peculiar people, and the only ones to receive a heavenly home with Jesus, Jehovah and the angels. [348] [349] (*See also Anointed, Bride of Christ, Little Flock, Remnant, The Christ, and The Church of Christ*)

---

[348] **Let God be True** (Watch Tower Bible & Tract Society, 1946) pp. 137, 138

[349] **Watch Tower Magazine** (Watch Tower Bible & Tract Society, August 15, 1996) p. 31